Praise for *Supercoach*

'Michael Neill, a supercoach in real life, has used his electrifying writing talent to cause this book to reach out and grab you by the shoulders and shake you till you wake up. I recommend it highly.'
STEVE CHANDLER, AUTHOR OF *100 WAYS TO MOTIVATE YOURSELF* AND *RIGHT NOW*

'Reading Supercoach is like having a reliable best friend on hand, passing on solid advice each time you read. How many "nuggets" does it take to make a gold mine? The answer in terms of wisdom is contained herein.'
ANDY FOWLER, EMMY AWARD-WINNING VISUAL-EFFECTS PRODUCER AND DIRECTOR OF VFX AT NETFLIX

'Michael Neill has a rare gift for blending theory and practice into an enjoyable and helpful read. Whether you're interested in coaching, being coached, or just thinking and smiling about your path through life, I recommend this book.'
DAVID GLAZER, FOUNDER AND LEADER, GOOGLE GENOMICS TEAM

'This book is one of the best, if not the best, book on coaching that I have ever read. What is so interesting about Supercoach is that you do not need to be a coach to benefit from reading it – you simply need to be alive. It is more than 250 pages of pure written gold. The stories, exercises, and "in a nutshell" summaries are simply powerful; and this book will be a gift to so many.'
STEVE HARDISON, PERSONAL, BUSINESS, AND RELATIONSHIP COACH, WWW.THEULTIMATECOACH.NET

'Michael has completely outdone even himself with this book. This is simply one of the best self-help books I've ever read, and certain to be a classic for years to come. Michael's words go straight to the heart. By reading this book, you will feel lighter, more joyful, and more able to enjoy this life in this moment.'
JENNIFER LOUDEN, AUTHOR OF *THE LIFE ORGANIZER* AND *THE WOMAN'S COMFORT BOOK*

'Supercoach is a perfect guide to help you navigate from thought to possibility to intention to results. This is much more than a "feel-good" read – this book is transformational. Read it and go make a difference!'
ROB OWEN, ADJUNCT PROFESSOR, THUNDERBIRD SCHOOL OF GLOBAL MANAGEMENT

'Supercoach is, indeed, super. Michael presents simple, actionable concepts that transform your relationship with goals, motivation, money, and life purpose. His tools are simple, but not always easy – but they're worth it. The exercises he includes are first-rate and have brought me a much richer life.'

STEVER ROBBINS, THE HOST OF THE #1 ITUNES BUSINESS PODCAST THE GET-IT-DONE GUY'S QUICK AND DIRTY TIPS TO WORK LESS AND DO MORE

'Success is such an intensely personal thing, it's almost impossible to define. But when we achieve it, whatever "it" is, we know it. Fortunately, there are a few among us whose gift is to help us make the transformation. Michael Neill is such a person. His success in teaching success has earned him the title "Supercoach," and he is a super writer, too – you won't find a better or more enjoyable way to discover your personal path to success than within the wise and wonderful pages of this extraordinary book. Bottom line? Read, heed … and succeed!'

LYNN A. ROBINSON, AUTHOR OF DIVINE INTUITION AND TRUST YOUR GUT

'Supercoach is turbocharged with simple, attainable lessons that cut to the heart of life's big issues. If you want to create a more meaningful experience of being alive, read this book!'

LAURA BERMAN FORTGANG, LIFE-COACHING PIONEER AND AUTHOR OF THE LITTLE BOOK ON MEANING

'In this simple yet profound book, Michael Neill shares the secrets of bringing a sense of ease and joy to the challenges of making lasting, profound changes in your life and the lives of those you work with.'

GAY HENDRICKS, PH.D., NEW YORK TIMES BESTSELLING AUTHOR OF THE BIG LEAP

'Michael Neill is the coach with X-ray vision, somehow able to see straight through the noise in your head to the heart of what makes for a better life. This book will be an inspiration to thousands and thousands of people.'

ROBERT HOLDEN, PH.D., AUTHOR OF HAPPINESS NOW! AND DIRECTOR OF SUCCESS INTELLIGENCE AND THE HAPPINESS PROJECT

'Every good coach knows that in order to coach, you must be coached. Supercoach is a coach's coach. Clear, simple, to the point and every tip gives you something to ponder. What a blessing!'

IYANLA VANZANT, #1 NEW YORK TIMES BESTSELLING AUTHOR AND TELEVISION PERSONALITY

SUPER COACH

Also by Michael Neill

Books

Feel Happy Now: Small Changes That Make a Huge Difference (2012, 2007)

You Can Have What You Want: Proven Strategies for Inner and Outer Success (2009, 2006)

The Inside-Out Trilogy:

The Inside-Out Revolution: The Only Thing You Need to Know to Change Your Life Forever (2013)

The Space Within: Finding Your Way Back Home (2016)

Creating the Impossible: A 90-Day Program to Get Your Dreams out of Your Head and into the World (2018)

CD programs

The Inside-Out Revolution: The Only Thing You Need to Know to Change Your Life Forever (audiobook, 2014)

Effortless Success: How to Get What You Want and Have a Great Time Doing It (6-CD set, 2011)

Online program

The Path to Effortless Change

SUPER COACH

10 Secrets to Transform
Anyone's Life

MICHAEL NEILL

HAY HOUSE

Carlsbad, California • New York City
London • Sydney • New Delhi

Published in the United Kingdom by:
Hay House UK Ltd, Astley House, 33 Notting Hill Gate, London W11 3JQ
Tel: +44 (0)20 3675 2450; Fax: +44 (0)20 3675 2451
www.hayhouse.co.uk

Published in the United States of America by:
Hay House Inc., PO Box 5100, Carlsbad, CA 92018-5100
Tel: (1) 760 431 7695 or (800) 654 5126
Fax: (1) 760 431 6948 or (800) 650 5115
www.hayhouse.com

Published and distributed in Australia by:
Hay House Australia Ltd, 18/36 Ralph St, Alexandria NSW 2015
Tel: (61) 2 9669 4299; Fax: (61) 2 9669 4144
www.hayhouse.com.au

Published and distributed in India by:
Hay House Publishers India, Muskaan Complex, Plot No.3, B-2,
Vasant Kunj, New Delhi 110 070
Tel: (91) 11 4176 1620; Fax: (91) 11 4176 1630; www.hayhouse.co.in

Text © Michael Neill, 2009, 2018

A version of the *West Side Story* text (*pages 25–26*) was first published in *Spirit & Destiny Soul Secrets* (Hay House UK, 2006).

The moral rights of the author have been asserted.

The information given in this book should not be treated as a substitute for professional medical advice; always consult a medical practitioner. Any use of information in this book is at the reader's discretion and risk. Neither the author nor the publisher can be held responsible for any loss, claim or damage arising out of the use, or misuse, of the suggestions made, the failure to take medical advice or for any material on third-party websites.

A catalogue record for this book is available from the British Library.

Tradepaper ISBN: 978-1-78817-162-5
E-book ISBN: 978-1-4019-2785-1

Interior images: 45, 47, 48, 106, 138, 170, 212 Michael Neill

To all the supercoaches, past and present, who have contributed their time, energy, love, and wisdom to creating a happier world.

'The only true voyage of discovery, the only fountain of Eternal Youth, would be not to visit strange lands but to possess other eyes, to behold the universe through the eyes of another, of a hundred others, to behold the hundred universes that each of them beholds, that each of them is...'

MARCEL PROUST

CONTENTS

FOREWORD

This was the sixth time someone had mentioned Michael Neill to me.

'Do you know Michael Neill? Have you read *Supercoach*? You should meet Michael.'

I was building Evercoach, a global community for coaches and educators, designed to help them coach better and build their businesses.

I had to get the book. I had to meet Michael.

As I sat and read through the original edition of *Supercoach*, I realized why so many people had encouraged me to read it. I felt moved and inspired by the simple secrets at the heart of the book. It was easy to read, yet profound in approach.

A few years later, I finally had the chance to meet Michael in person. Sitting at a café on a sunny day in Santa Monica, California, sipping our Bulletproof Coffee, we had a heart to heart about the world of coaching. We talked about everything – structures, challenges, and potential solutions.

After the meeting, I knew one thing for sure: Michael was exactly what you'd hope he would be from reading the book and a shining example of how a supercoach approaches coaching.

So when he asked me to read the new edition, I was both excited and a little nervous. Why change what had already become a classic in the field?

Human beings are among the greatest creators to walk on this planet. We create the greatest inventions, and we also create our own realities. Often these realities are influenced by what is happening outside us. We are influenced by those we are with – friends, family, colleagues. We react to the world – politics, the economy, the environment. It's like being in a boxing ring where all we do is defend ourselves in order not to get punched.

While constantly on the defense, how can we learn to play, as Michael says, 'full out and fearless'? How can we create a winning strategy when all our energy is focused on trying not to lose?

I've been in that boxing ring for too much of my life. As it happened, the week the book arrived I found myself once again caught up in the feeling of not being enough, struggling with the challenge of constantly comparing myself with my ideal self and where I thought I 'should' be, given everything I've learned and everything I've done.

As I started reading, I remembered why I had fallen in love with the first edition and I realized why I needed to read the book again. I had innocently become so lost in my 'reality' that I needed it to remind me of who and what I really was. I also realized why Michael had rewritten it – to make it even more accessible to even more people.

There is an innate truth about life that we already know inside ourselves – that we are perfect and whole as we are, and that we will continually forget that fact. We already know inside ourselves everything we need to know. We are the teacher we need. We are the coach that we need.

This book will show you how to unleash your inner coach as well as remind you of some simple truths about life. What it did for me when I needed it most is what I hope it will do for you in the coming hours…

Have you ever been in a place where you compared yourself to someone else, or to where you 'should' be in relation to your goals?

Has there ever been a time when you felt you didn't have enough money, or enough love, that your boss didn't care, or that your friends weren't giving you enough attention?

Does a lack of creativity feel like a constant challenge?

Are you giving everything you have but feeling like nothing that you do is good enough?

This new edition of *Supercoach* will help you with all these things and much, much more.

As you go through the ten sessions, I invite you to stop once in a while. Reflect. This book is not a just an enjoyable read that you can finish in an afternoon and then add to your bookshelf like a trophy. It's a personal coach that you can call on in times of challenge – and in times of wonder. It's a portable coach that will stand beside you through good times and bad, offering you exactly what you need at the exact moment you need it.

If you're searching for a competitive advantage in your career , read this book.

If you're looking for a better life, read this book.

If you're wanting to be a supercoach for yourself, for others, and for our planet…

Read. This. Book.

AJIT NAWALKHA
Co-founder, Evercoach & Mindvalley Teach

PREFACE:
TEN YEARS LATER...

In the early years of a coaching career that has now spanned three decades, I often saw myself as 'a preacher in search of a gospel.' I knew I was gifted with the ability to say things in a way that people could hear; I just wasn't always sure I had anything particularly worth saying.

That all changed in the 18 months or so leading up to writing the original version of *Supercoach*. I'd come across a book by Dr George Pransky called *The Relationship Handbook*, and I was sufficiently intrigued by what I'd read to go and visit him in the Pacific Northwest and spend some time working with one of his colleagues, Dr Keith Blevens. To my surprise, I had what I can only describe as a spiritual epiphany while I was there, and it changed me at a fundamental level. Before that moment, I had been a 'high-functioning depressive'; after that moment, I was genuinely happy in a way I hadn't been since I was a young child.

At first I thought I'd finally found 'my gospel,' but after a time I came to see that what I had actually found was even better than that: I'd found that space inside myself (and all human beings) that could be seen as the source of all gospels.

Because I wasn't remotely religious and was in fact uncomfortable with all things spiritual, I set about writing about what I'd experienced in a way that I thought would still maintain my 'street cred' as a hyper-rational man of the world. My first attempt at putting words to the indescribable feelings was in the form of a novella. To my surprise, both my wife and my publisher asked me not to bring it out, as they felt it was too much of a leap from my previous work. It remains unpublished. Downhearted but not defeated, I got on a plane with a couple of friends from the entertainment industry and got rip-snortingly drunk.

On one of my many subsequent trips to the restroom, a new book started writing itself in my head. It would be built around 10 insights, or secrets, and would share what I was seeing about the human potential in the form of a coaching conversation with an imaginary client. I raced back to my seat and began taking notes. Around 2 a.m. the next morning, wide awake with jet-lag and creative adrenaline, I opened up my computer, typed up my notes, and sent them off to my agent. When I next opened my computer, around 8 a.m., I was surprised to see an email from him saying that he had sent the notes off to Hay House and they had offered to publish the book when it was written.

The book was a hit, and it led to my starting an international coach training school called Supercoach Academy, which has now trained people from over 40 countries in the art and science of transformative coaching. And as my understanding of the principles I had first shared in *Supercoach* evolved, I wrote a trilogy of books elucidating them further: *The Inside-Out Revolution*, *The Space Within*, and *Creating the Impossible*.

So why do a revised and updated edition of *Supercoach*?

One of my early mentors, the co-founder of neuro-linguistic programming (NLP) and prolific author Dr Richard Bandler, used to say, 'There are people all over the world stuck at various stages of my personal development.' He was referring to the fact that while he was continually learning and evolving both in himself and his work, wherever he went there were people holding up his earlier writings as 'the truth' and wondering why he had changed his mind.

In my own life, I noticed myself cringing a little whenever people came up to me and thanked me for writing *Supercoach*. While I had thought it to be a definitive work at the time that I wrote it, in subsequent visits to the text I began to see that the book was an inadvertent hybrid of the kind of empowering self-help books I had written early in my career and the new, nascent understanding I was attempting to articulate.

I began rewriting sections of the book, not for publication but as a resource for my clients and students. After sharing a few of these sections more widely and receiving extremely positive feedback, I mentioned to my agent that I was thinking of rewriting the whole manuscript. Less than 72 hours later, he emailed to say that Hay House was once again interested in publishing the book when it was written.

Early on during the rewriting process I made the decision that rather than start from scratch, I would attempt to keep as much of the original text as I could. So, if you were a fan of the original version, you'll be pleased to find many of the ideas and stories from the original work peppered throughout this one. But some sections required complete excision from the manuscript, while others required new stories and explanations, both to bridge the gaps in the narrative and to flesh out the key points I was trying to make.

So, two pieces of advice before you begin:

1. If you're completely new to the book, just enjoy it. I trust that you will find it enlightening, and that as you read, your experience of life will begin to change for the better, often without effort and sometimes even without being able to point to a particular reason why.

2. If you read the original, or are a fan of any of the 100-plus books that have emerged in the field of the Three Principles since *Supercoach* was first published back in 2009, I encourage you to see this for what it is – a gentle introduction to some game-changing truths about life, designed for people who want to better their own lives and make more of a positive difference in the world.

Have fun, learn heaps, and happy exploring!

With all my love,

Michael

Introduction

A DIFFERENT WAY TO SUCCEED

What if, regardless of your past history or the current economy, your dreams really could come true?

What would you be most excited about having happen in your life over the next few weeks, months, or years? Would you like to experience dramatic breakthroughs in your career, business, or finances? Deeper love and connection in your relationships? How about seemingly miraculous improvements in your levels of health and wellbeing?

For the past 30 years or so, I've been a professional life coach – someone who gets paid to help make people's dreams come true. In that time, I've learned that not only are there many different types of dreams, there are all sorts of different ways to realize them.

Whether you want to make more money, build your business, start a family, or save the world, chances are that your approach up until now has been primarily practical – that is, focused on what it is you want and what it is you think you need to do in order to make it happen. If you're a reasonably progressive thinker, you're probably also aware that one of the reasons you want what you want is that you believe it will in some way enhance your experience of being alive. But, as you may have already begun to realize, if you really want to have a more enjoyable life, reaching your goals isn't necessarily going to do it. First and foremost, you're going to have to find a more enjoyable way to live.

This is a book about living from the inside out. As you learn to live more in tune with your deepest wisdom, stress disappears and worry becomes almost non-existent. You realize that you were born happy and the worst thing that can ever happen to you is a thought – generally speaking, a thought about whatever you think is the worst thing that could ever happen to you. Things still won't always work out as you'd hoped or planned, but that just becomes a fact of life instead of a problem to be solved. And since you spend more of your time in a state of being full (of life, joy, love, and peace), going outside yourself to 'find fulfillment' loses most of its appeal.

Of course, that doesn't mean you won't still do all sorts of weird and wonderful things with your life. It just means that you'll be allowing what's inside you to create things on the outside instead of trying to do them the other way around.

So how can a coach help?

THE THREE LEVELS OF CHANGE

'All miracles involve a shift in perception.'
A Course in Miracles

People hire coaches for one simple reason: they want to get more out of themselves and their lives than they seem to be getting on their own.

For example, why are you reading this?

Chances are that you're looking for something to help you change your life for the better – to improve your circumstances, or make you feel better, or bring you closer to your essential nature. You're thinking to yourself, *There has to be a better way of being in the world than the way I'm going about it.* You're hoping that what I'm going to share with you will give you more of a sense of meaning, value, and purpose and help you enjoy success in multiple areas of your life.

As a transformative coach, I begin with the premise that the starting-point for all life-enhancement projects is a deeper understanding of the nature of the human experience. People will naturally get more out of themselves when they understand more about who they are and how the human system works. They'll automatically get more out of their lives when they gain more insight into how life works. Because when we really understand how something works, from a sliding door to a car to gravity, we don't have to think about it anymore and can just get on with it. We slide, drive, and even fall to the ground with a sense of ease and simplicity.

In the same way, when we know who we really are and where our experience comes from, we don't have to overthink things. We can live our lives and follow our wisdom knowing that when we're up, we're up, when we're down, we're down, and love, peace, connection, and insight are available all the time, regardless of how we're feeling.

In other words, if there's something you want to create or do in the world, knowing how things actually get created and done is of universal benefit. All boats will rise with the tide of that deeper understanding.

Traditional coaching takes place primarily in a horizontal dimension – coaches assist their clients in getting from point A to point B. Yet lasting change nearly always happens in the vertical dimension – a deepening of the client's ground of being and greater access to inspiration and inner wisdom. While this has generally led to an either/or approach to success and personal growth and a sharp division between therapy and coaching, transformative coaching (or, as I like to call it, 'supercoaching') uses the vertical dimension to facilitate change on the inside even as you continue to move toward your goals on the outside.

The kinds of changes that transformative coaching leads to can be usefully viewed on three levels…

Level I: Change in a specific situation

Often people will hire a coach (or go to a counselor, therapist, or friend) to get help with a specific situation they're struggling with. They may want to deal with a difficult person at work, succeed at an important negotiation or job interview, or stay motivated as they train to beat their personal best at a sporting event. This kind of performance coaching has long been a staple of the industry, and long before 'life coaching' and 'executive coaching' became common terms, people were using coaches in this capacity to help change their points of view, states of mind, or actions. At this level, people go from fear to confidence, from unease to comfort, or from inaction to action.

The impact of this kind of coaching is generally project specific. Once the difficult person has been handled, the interview completed, or the race run, people get on with the rest of their lives in much the same way as they did before.

Level II: Change in a specific life area

Sometimes we're less concerned with a specific event than we are with a whole category of events. This is why we find coaches specializing in any number of life areas: relationships, sales, parenting, confidence, presentations … the list goes on and on. People hire these experts to help them increase their skills and develop their confidence in the area they are having difficulty with.

Like performance coaches, these coaches will help with specific situations, but they tend to measure their impact not just by how one situation changes, but by how a whole category of situations changes.

Level III: Transformation

The ultimate level of change is transformation, or what I sometimes call 'global change' – a pervasive shift in our understanding and way of being in the world. At this level, it's not enough for us to develop a skill or change a feeling. We want to see our higher potential and wake up from the dream of thought, because in so doing our experience of everything changes and we begin to walk in a different world.

◆

Each of the three levels maps across to a certain way of working on ourselves or with others. When we want to make a change in a specific situation, we apply a new technique. When we want to make a change in a broader context, we apply a new strategy. But when we want to transform our life, we need something other than techniques or strategies – we need to see what's true about life so that we can live more in harmony with how things actually work.

How else do the three levels of change differ?

Well, the first two levels are primarily intervention based. Level I interventions take care of the presenting problem, while Level II interventions aim to take care of whatever is seen as the underlying cause. This can be helpful, but it can also lead people deeper into the morass of their own psychology. For example, people heavily into personal development sometimes get fixated on finding Level II solutions for Level I problems – they've got a headache, but instead of taking an aspirin, they want to analyze the lifestyle changes they need to make to become the kind of person who doesn't get headaches. It's an interesting idea, but it's a lot easier to do when your head isn't hurting.

At Level III, you're simply looking to see what's true for all human beings, regardless of individual differences. And while you may still take the aspirin, knowing that everyone gets headaches and they invariably pass takes the pressure off you to fix it.

The Three Levels in Action

Let's look at a couple of examples in more depth.

Bob is a customer service rep for a medium-sized manufacturing firm, and he's having a really bad day. When I ask him what his biggest sticking point is, he tells me it's a phone call he needs to make to a supplier in Detroit with whom he's been having difficulties.

If I were to approach this on Level I, I might work with his frame of mind by helping him get into a more confident state. We might role-play a phone call with his supplier, and I might offer him tips and techniques to better handle the call and get the outcome he most wants. We might even choose to script the call, or at least the beginning of it, to help boost his confidence and resolve the situation.

But let's say I want more for Bob – I don't just want to assist him in getting through this one situation, I want to help turn him into a more effective employee, one who can handle a wider variety of customer service situations. So I give him books like *How to Talk So People Listen*. I teach him rapport skills like 'matching and mirroring' so he can use body language to effectively allow others to feel more comfortable around him.

What then? In time and with practice, Bob might be able to turn things around and maybe even become the best customer service guy in the whole company. But in another way, nothing will have really changed. Because in order for something to change at a fundamental level, that change has to happen via an *insight* – a sight from within.

So at the level of transformation, our conversation will no longer be about the supplier from Detroit, or even about customer service. Our 'transformative conversation' might be about the nature of satisfaction and dissatisfaction – what they are and where they come from. Or we may go even deeper to look at the nature of what it is to be alive. In exploring these universal truths, Bob will get insights and fresh thinking that change the way he sees himself, the way he sees his job, and the way he sees other people. And through those insights, he'll not only become more effective in his job, he'll also become more satisfied and effective in his life.

Here's another example, one that might hit closer to home. Imagine you're having difficulties with your resident teenager. You want them to help out around the house and be more respectful toward you and your partner, but they seem determined to set a new world record for most dirty clothes piled up in one corner of a bedroom.

At Level I, you could go in guns a-blazing and order them to pick up their dirty clothes 'or else.' You might even try a subtler approach – the dangling carrot of concert tickets or a shopping trip to the nearest mall in exchange for a cleaner room.

At Level II, you might read parenting books on how to handle discipline problems with teens, or even business books on how to handle difficult people at work in the hope that you could map it across to your own child at home. (Of course, if you come across a copy of *What to Do When You Work for an Idiot* in their bedroom, chances are they're planning a little Level II intervention with you!)

But at Level III, the level of transformation, you would know that the difference that would really make a difference was insight – a shift in consciousness that comes about through looking within ('in-sight') to see a deeper truth about how life works.

For example, when my daughter Clara was six, she went through a period of violent temper tantrums that frightened her teachers to the point where they were considering either putting her on medication or kicking her out of school. My wife and I had no clue what to do about it, so we turned to one of my mentors, Bill Cumming.

His coaching addressed all three levels simultaneously. At Level I, he continually checked in with us to ensure that we were doing okay within ourselves – that is, we were getting adequate sleep, food, and exercise, and doing whatever else we needed for what he called our 'spiritual self-care.'

At Level II, he shared some wonderful strategies for dealing with difficult children. The one that sticks in my mind is the two 'C's: *clarity* and *consistency*. We got clear about what was and wasn't okay, and more consistent in our enforcement of those rules.

But in all honesty, other than taking our minds off the problem and focusing us on what we could actually do instead of everything that might go wrong, I'm not sure that those things made much of a difference. What has stayed with us to this day, however, was *insight* from our conversations into where Clara's behavior was coming from and the nature of unconditional love. It became obvious to us that the only reason someone would behave in the way Clara was behaving was if they felt unwell within themselves. Her behavior was actually an attempt to self-soothe and make herself feel better.

As we began to see the discomfort in Clara that was leading to her acting out, it became much easier not to take her behavior personally, as though it was her way of punishing us for our parenting failures. More important, any catastrophizing we'd been doing in our heads about how this would be a problem for the rest of her life, and 'if it's this bad now, imagine how bad it will be when she's a teenager,' fell away. We began to see her as a little girl doing the best she could to manage her feelings, in this instance by controlling her environment through a reign of six-year-old terror. We knew that when she was less scared of her own feelings, her innate wisdom and common sense would guide her forward. That made it easy and natural to feel the full force of our love for her, even when she was behaving in ways that were shocking and at times a little bit frightening for us.

It no longer made sense to me to send her to her room when she had a tantrum in a behaviorist effort to 'extinguish' the unwanted behavior. What it occurred to me to do was to go into her room with her and just quietly be with her as she worked through whatever it was she was working through.

At first, she didn't seem to like this new approach. Instead of simply putting holes in the walls of her bedroom, she seemed hell-bent on putting a few in my head. But after a few tantrums, she somehow recognized that she was safe, even when she was suffering from the mental clutter and discomfort that affect all of us from time to time. That feeling of safety allowed her natural wisdom, clarity, and wellbeing to come back to the fore.

Now, as a young adult, Clara is more secure in herself and her thinking than most people I know. And while we certainly had our share of issues during her teenage years, the closeness we felt and the insight we gleaned when she was six went a long way to seeing us through them.

TEN SESSIONS TO TRANSFORM YOUR LIFE

'Men occasionally stumble over the truth, but most of them pick themselves up and hurry off as if nothing had happened.'
WINSTON CHURCHILL

This book is laid out in 10 coaching sessions, each one built around a 'secret' understanding about life. We could call these secrets 'guidelines,' in the sense that they will reliably guide us through the uncharted territory of life; we could also call them 'understandings,' in the sense that once we understand them, we'll never relate to our problems, goals, or the people in our lives in the same way again.

Each session is designed to be a catalyst for you – something that will spark your own insights about your work, your finances, your relationships, and yourself. An insight is something that once seen can never be unseen. That's why there's nothing here to master and no particular skills or techniques to learn.

What makes most change seem difficult is that we're trying to do it from the outside in – that is, to change our behavior on the outside without any change in how we're seeing the situation on the inside. Because there's no internal basis for making the change, we need external motivation, reminders, and any other threats and bribes we can think of in order to consistently behave in the ways that we or someone else has decided are good for us. But the moment we see things differently, either because we have more information or we've had some kind of insight, change is natural, effortless, and inevitable.

Let's imagine for a moment that you travel to work each weekday morning. And let's pretend that it's a fairly unpleasant commute – it takes upward of an hour there and back, and there's either a lot of traffic at that time of day or the train is inevitably packed, or both. Now, let's say I happen to know a shortcut you could take that would enable you to get to work and back in no more than 15 minutes. Better still, the journey would be pleasant, uncrowded, and rather beautiful. How many times would I have to show you the new route before you began taking it as a matter of course?

It wouldn't matter if you'd been doing things in the old way for years, or if you had low self-esteem or had had a difficult childhood. The moment you saw that this new route was a genuinely better way to get where you wanted to go, you'd begin to take it. The entire experience would be effortless, because the external change (your new behavior) would be the natural fruit of the internal shift – your new understanding of what was possible.

In a similar way, each session in this book will enable you to see a number of 'shortcuts' to happiness, success, and wellbeing.

And as your understanding of what's possible grows, your life will begin to change for the better, all by itself.

How to Get the Most Out of This Book

'Don't cut the person to fit the cloth.'
Sufi saying

In these pages, we'll be taking a deep dive together into the largely uncharted waters of the human potential. We'll be focusing less on 'how to live' than on a new understanding of how life works – an understanding that will lead to your taking new actions in your life and appreciating new possibilities in the lives of the people you care about most.

The foundation of that dive is exploring what's true for all human beings, regardless of their upbringing or circumstances. When we can really see what we have going for us (and what we're up against) in the realm of creating results, high performance, and a life well-lived, we can point others to that same potential (and those same obstacles) in themselves.

So perhaps the most effective way to use this book would be to read through it cover to cover, then go back and spend a week or so playing with the ideas in each session. But then again, perhaps not.

Each person is unique, and the value you'll get from reading this book will be found more in the insights it provokes than the actual content or exercises. In other words, you may get everything you need in one reading, but if you find yourself wanting more, it's designed to stand up to deeper inspection and introspection.

One of the many things that emerge from this kind of reflection over time is a clearer sense of what's on offer, codified into three objectives that build on one another to make for a truly wonderful life...

1. To come alive to the magnificence inside us

For the past few years, my business one-liner has been 'Unleashing the human potential with intelligence, humor, and heart.' While the 'intelligence, humor, and heart' bit is perhaps self-explanatory, I always find it interesting that the idea of 'human potential' is both widely accepted and largely underestimated.

In his foreword to *The Inside-Out Revolution*, my friend and mentor Dr George Pransky talks about it like this:

> *Everyone experiences times of mental clarity and wellbeing, even moments of out and out genius. Even in the extremes of mental illness, every single patient has moments of 'normalcy' independent of the severity of their disorder. At a more personal level, we have all come up with inspirations and solutions that seem to have shown up out of nowhere to save the day. At times, our children's wisdom goes way beyond their level of education and life experience. And we consistently see high levels of wellbeing, grace, and hopefulness emerge in times of crisis such as floods and earthquakes, and even with people informed of terminal illnesses. So it should be equally obvious that*

*the human potential for life enjoyment, mental clarity,
creativity, and relationship satisfaction is considerably
higher than we are manifesting in our everyday lives.*

As we come alive to our 'inner spark,' we start to move through the world with greater ease and a less conditional sense of confidence and wellbeing. While our life circumstances may still seem messy from time to time, people can't help but notice a twinkle in our eye and a lovely feeling in our presence. Here's how I go on to describe it in the book:

*Some people describe this transformative shift as moving
from riding a roller coaster to floating in a river; others as
the gift of meeting themselves for the first time. 'It's as if I've
been plugged back into the mains,' one client said to me. By
far the most common description is some variation on the
feeling of coming home after a long time away. While your
experience will be unique to you, the awakening of your
inner spark and a feeling of reconnection with the energy of
life are part of the promise and purpose of our time together.*

2. To go beyond our psychology

I had a friend who trained as a traditional psychologist but developed a somewhat unusual premise: that every human being has a personal psychology, and that all personal psychologies are inherently neurotic and insecure. While I didn't necessarily agree with her conclusions about what to do about it, I don't dispute the premise.

Our 'psychology' in this sense is a catch-all phrase for the sum total of our habitual thinking – what might in other contexts be called our personality, our conditioned self, or our ego. And there are a few things that seem to me to be true across the board about our psychology:

♦ we all have one and get caught up in it from time to time

♦ a certain amount of the thinking we have could accurately be described as 'neurotic' and/or 'insecure'

and most importantly:

♦ we are *not* our psychology – we are the thinker, not the sum total of our thoughts.

And it is this last point that points us toward a different way of being with our psychology. If I am the thinker, not the thoughts, then I don't have to overcome or 'fix' my thoughts and feelings. They will come and go as all ephemera do. And in noticing the temporary nature of my thought-created story of my past and my thought-created future hopes and fears, I also begin to notice that which is constant and unchanging – the inner spark and wisdom within that make up the human potential.

3. To create cool stuff in the world

When we don't create to sate our psychology but to satisfy the incredibly human urge to facilitate the divine creative force taking form, it's remarkable how much we can actually get done without exhaustion, stress, or pressure. And when we take things one step at a time without feeling the need to bite off more than we can chew (or do more than we're capable of doing and control more than we're actually in control of), it's remarkable how many of those steps take us far further than we imagined they would.

One of my favorite descriptions of what happens when you begin to live from a deeper understanding of life is what I often talk about as 'effortless success.' 'Effortless,' in this instance, isn't about an avoidance of physical work; it's about an absence of mental struggle. Happiness leads to success, wellbeing leads to inspiration, and success and inspiration become the basis for an ever more wonderful life.

At some point, people come to see that creating effortless success isn't magic (although it certainly is magical) – it's the natural result of approaching life from a place of profound wellbeing, listening for the inner call, and following it wherever it leads.

In the words of Henry David Thoreau:

> If one advances confidently in the direction of his dreams, and endeavors to live the life which he has imagined, he will meet with a success unexpected in common hours.

So let's look directly at you for a moment. Are you:

♦ Struggling to move forward? Moving forward by struggling?

♦ Experiencing wonderful results and happy accidents but secretly worrying about when the magic is going to stop, when the batteries are going to run out, or how you'll ever be able to apply this to 'the big stuff' in your life?

◆   Living life at peace in yourself (mostly), but wondering if
     and when you're ever going to get in the game and make
     your dreams come true?

Wherever you currently are, you can use the 10 sessions in
this book to assist with your transition – from struggle to ease,
from ease to peace, and from peace to power. As you set your
direction, rest in wellbeing, and listen for the whispers of your
own inner wisdom, you'll be amazed by how easy that transition
will be.

Your journey begins just as soon as you turn this page...

Session One

THE ART OF DREAMING

'Life is a divine dream, suspended between the boundaries of time, space, and matter.'

Syd Banks

THE STONECUTTER AND THE ANGEL

Once upon a time there was a young stonecutter who looked with envy upon the rich merchant who employed him. One day he was muttering to himself about what it would be like to have such freedom and power when, to his amazement, an angel appeared and spoke the words: 'You are as you have thought.' In an instant, the stonecutter had become the merchant.

He was very happy with his lot until he saw the king of the land ride by with his coterie. *Now that's the way to live*, he thought.

Almost before he had asked, the angel had granted his wish and the merchant had become the king.

All was well until one beautiful summer's day when the king began sweating in his heavy royal garb. *What freedom and power the sun has*, he thought. *It can float through the sky and call forth water from a king. That is what I would truly like to be.*

As the thought appeared in his mind, the angel appeared to grant it.

Now the king had become the sun, and he reveled in his freedom and power as he floated high above the Earth. But after a time, a cloud appeared and blocked the land from his view. When he watched the lightning burst forth from the cloud and heard the roar of the thunder, he knew that he was witnessing true freedom and power. Before he even realized what was happening, the angel had transformed him into a cloud.

What fun it was to pour rain forth upon the land! Wherever the man–cloud went, forests were washed away, and puddles became oceans in his wake. But no matter how hard he tried, there was one huge mountain made of stone that stood immovable and unaffected by his rain.

Surely that is the ultimate power, he thought. To stand tall in the face of any circumstance – that is true freedom and power.

In an instant, the angel had made it so, and the man could feel the incredible power of being immovable in the midst of any storm. Yet even as he was delighting in his immense strength and resilience, he could see a small man chipping away at his base with a pick and a chisel and a hammer.

That man is even more powerful than I am, he thought. See how he is able to take stone away from me with just a few blows of his mighty tools. That is the kind of freedom and power I have always longed for.

The angel appeared and once again spoke the words, 'You are as you have thought.'

And with those words, the older but wiser stonecutter continued on his journey.

THE POWER OF MAKE-BELIEVE

I began acting when I was six years old; at the age of 12, I played Hamlet. But the experience that launched my quest for understanding the human psyche didn't come until I was 15 and was playing Pepe, a Puerto Rican gang member, in a youth-theater production of *West Side Story*.

Now there's a musical number fairly early on in the show called 'Dance at the Gym.' And this was the first chance we Puerto Ricans really got to strut our stuff. The choreography was sexy, very Latin, and noisy – lots of shouting of '*Ay, Caramba*' and '*Chee, Chee, Chee*' and other approximations of what a bunch of suburban white kids imagined Puerto Rican gang members would say.

This was my favorite part of the show, and that particular night we really got into it. We danced until the sweat was pouring and the lights were hot and the girls were hot and the music was hot and it felt as though the whole theater was burning up. We were all riding that passion and feeling those really intense feelings, and then we got into the scene called the Rumble. Well, we'd done this dozens of times before. The Americans taunted us, we taunted them, there was a lot of macho dancing with switchblades, and in the end, Bernardo stabbed Riff and we all ran like hell. Only this time, something different happened.

One of the American gang members, a big blond guy named Snowball, was looking at me, and he started calling out, '*Ay, Caramba!*' and '*Chee, Chee, Chee*,' and making fun of the way we'd been dancing in the previous scene. And all of a sudden I went from hot to furious. Not pretend, not acting – genuinely furious.

Now I don't know if you've ever been made fun of because of your race, appearance, gender, or sexuality, but I was so filled with anger at that moment that I wanted to leap across the stage and kill him.

Fortunately for both of us, there was a curious part of me that was observing the whole scene and offering up some useful counterarguments. First, I'm not Puerto Rican. Second, the actor playing Snowball was actually a good friend I hung out with offstage. Third, we weren't on the mean streets of New York City – we were in a theater in a small town in Massachusetts, doing a play in front of a few hundred people.

Yet the anger I felt when the person he was pretending to be insulted the person I was pretending to be was red-hot and real.

What I came to realize that night is that if you 'make believe' something long enough (like being a Puerto Rican gang member), it becomes real to you – you begin to think and feel and act as if it's true. Otherwise I would never have been upset about being teased for being Puerto Rican. (Let's face it, assuming you're not one, if someone called you a 'stupid tuna fish' you probably wouldn't take it personally.)

This brings me to the secret we'll be exploring in this session. It's the secret that underpins everything else we'll be doing together, because it explains why we see what we see, hear what we hear, feel what we feel, and do what we do. It's a secret that has been talked about in many eras and many traditions from around the world and is 'secret' not because no one wants you to know it, but because it's so difficult to talk about – like trying to explain the concept of water to a fish.

The secret is that we live in a world of thought, not circumstances. The mind works like a projector, not a camera, which is to say we experience what we think, not some kind of 'objective reality.'

If you're having a wonderful experience, that experience is coming to you via thought. If you're having a horrible experience, well, that's made of thought too.

The wonderful thing about thought is that it can change in a heartbeat. And once you really begin to understand how your thoughts create your 'reality,' you'll no longer be a victim of the process.

Or to put it more succinctly:

> Your world is what you think it is, but
> there's a world beyond your thinking.

My initial understanding of this secret came from insights I gleaned while studying the teachings of a Scottish welder named Syd Banks, who had an enlightenment experience at the age of 43. While writing about what he saw could fill volumes (and indeed has), here's one of his simplest articulations, which includes this first secret:

I had this experience and I realized it was a world of thought. Because whatever we think is what we feel, whatever we think is what we see, whatever we think creates our desires. It creates good marriages, bad marriages. But there is a greater secret than that. You step beyond the five senses, and when you learn to step beyond the five senses you live a happy, contented life full of love. Because love is always the answer.

Syd talked about life in terms of three principles – irreducible elements out of which everything in life is created. While he described each of them in hundreds of different ways, here are some of his more concise descriptions to give us a starting-point for our exploration:

♦ '*Mind* is the intelligence of literally all things in this world or any other world… [It's] the Mind that has the power to guide you through life.'

♦ '*Consciousness* gives us the ability to realize the existence of life… Consciousness is infinite – there is no end to it.'

♦ '*Thought* is a gift we were given to have the freedom to walk through life and see what we want to see… Thought is not reality, yet it is through Thought that our realities are created.'

He then went on to put them together in two simple ways, one mathematical and one poetic in its simplicity:

♦ 'Mind + Consciousness + Thought = Reality'

♦ 'Our thoughts are the camera, our eyes are the lens. Put them together and the picture we see is reality.'

Here's how it looks to me and why I've found it to be so important as a starting-point for any coaching conversation...

For a painter to become more effective at creating art, they first need to understand the basic principles of painting – color, texture, perspective, and line. Of course, simply understanding these principles will not cause their next painting to be a universally acclaimed masterpiece, but it will make it far more likely that over time their work will become better and better and they'll find more and more joy in its creation.

In the same way, if you want to be more effective at the art of living, it's important to understand the principles behind life.

So, let's look at each of the three principles in a bit more depth...

THE THREE PRINCIPLES

The Principle of Mind

Regardless of whether you use scientific or spiritual language to describe it, *the principle of Mind* points to the oneness of life – the energy that runs through everything like an animating spirit, invisibly bringing things to life like the electricity that stands ready to power any device we might choose to plug into it. It is pure potential, indiscriminately empowering whatever thoughts we drop into it like the lamp of a projector indiscriminately projecting the shadow of whatever passes in front of it onto a screen.

I often refer to the intersection of that universal force with our individual biology as 'the deeper mind.' While sometimes it seems as though it exists outside us, we can no more be separate from it than an individual wave can be separate from the ocean of which it is a part.

The Principle of Consciousness

What allows us to experience the oneness of life is *the principle of Consciousness* – the capacity we all have to experience our own individual version of the unchanging whole. Consciousness – that within us that allows us to be consciously aware of something – is like a mirror, reflecting whatever passes in front of it without being affected by it. It is the space within – the sky through which birds fly and inside which clouds come and go.

I sometimes refer to Consciousness more colloquially as 'bandwidth,' or even 'headspace,' as it often seems to expand or contract throughout the day.

The Principle of Thought

The principle of Thought is pure creative potential, bringing form out of the formless like, in Syd's words, 'a magical paintbrush.' Thought is the pure spiritual energy through which both our habitual thinking and our inspired ideas come to mind. It is the playdough of the universe, and we use it to create monsters and demons and heavens and angels with equal frequency.

If source energy is the paint, the principle of Thought is the (magical) paintbrush. Our life is the canvas, and our consciousness is what allows us to appreciate the painting. Because different thoughts come in and out of our head throughout the day, our experience is continually changing. But because we tend to focus on the same limited range of thoughts throughout the day, there is a sense of cohesive reality to our experience.

Of course, just because a thought pops into your head doesn't mean it will immediately manifest in the world of form. (If it did, there would be more deaths by rollercoasters going off their tracks, people falling from very high places, and heads exploding due to stress than any other cause.) That's because in and of themselves, thoughts have no power. It's only when you breathe life into them that they begin to seem real. A thought without personal investment is no more powerful than a tea bag without boiling water. It's only after you add the water that the tea begins to infuse and create the flavor, and it's only after you add your agreement and energy to a thought that it begins to impact your life.

What makes thoughts appear to be so powerful is that the more we invest our attention in them, the more 'real' they start to feel. This is why positive thinking so often backfires – it enlivens thoughts by making them into 'things' that must be avoided or pursued. Simply noticing the energy of Thought arising, taking form, and fading away back into nothingness will nearly always lead to a better quality of experience than bringing in the 'thought police' to try to control errant thoughts.

When we unwittingly create more demons than angels without noticing that they flow forth from the same pen, we struggle; when we deliberately orient our thoughts toward the positive, we enjoy our lives more; when we see beyond both positive and negative to the space of pure Consciousness that contains them, the energy of Thought that creates them, and the animating force of Mind that brings them to life, we thrive.

THE PRINCIPLES IN ACTION

While I hope you're getting a sense of these universal energies as I'm describing them, I know that reading even the best description of how life works will no more change your life for the better than reading a beautifully written menu will satisfy your hunger. So, in pointing out these invisible forces, I often point first to their *effects* – like explaining electricity by switching on a lamp or demonstrating gravity by dropping a pen to the floor. And the easiest place for many of us to see Mind, Thought, and Consciousness in action is in seeing how our experience of a particular life event can change over time, and even moment by moment:

♦ Our bank balance is what it is, yet the power of Thought can make it seem like a lot or a little, nowhere near or far more than enough. And as we feel our thinking, it brings with it temporary feelings of security or insecurity, happiness or sadness, excitement or fear.

♦ Our thinking is what it is, but depending on our level of consciousness at the time, we get lost in the feelings it brings or see them for what they are – an ever-changing movement of energy against the constant backdrop of our deeper nature. Depending on our level of understanding, the thought/feeling system can drag us around by the nose or appear as a fascinating movement within the stillness of our nature.

♦ Our level of consciousness is what it is, but the constant spark of Mind is always burning, keeping our heart beating, lungs breathing, and brain thinking as we go about our lives.

By way of analogy, think of your brain as operating like a laptop hooked into a kind of universal internet. The universal internet (i.e. the principle of Mind) is the energy and intelligence of life coming through you and to you. Everything that appears on your screen is made up of the energy of Thought; what determines the ease of flow of Thought is your mental bandwidth (i.e. the principle of Consciousness).

Bandwidth is by nature infinite, but the range of what we see expands and contracts on a regular basis. When our bandwidth is high, we can process information quickly and easily, handle multiple tasks simultaneously and efficiently, and our experience is one of ease and flow. When our bandwidth is low, everything slows down, nothing works quite as designed, and we experience a fair bit of mental 'buffering' where we can't quite get our head around where we left our keys, let alone how to run a business, score a goal, or have a helpful conversation with our clients and colleagues.

Within the analogy, there are two things worth knowing about bandwidth. The first is that we have no direct control over it – it expands and contracts on its own. The second is that the more we understand the relationship between bandwidth and mental clarity, the less inclined we are to fill it up with lots of extra thinking, no matter how positive that thinking might be.

Plato's Cave for a New Millennium

To better understand the implications of this secret, imagine you're sitting in a theater watching a scary movie. The movie is well made, and you get caught up in it to the point where you physically shrink back into your seat when the pretty girl heads down the dark stairway with an old flashlight whose batteries mysteriously stop working as soon as she hears a strange creaking sound from the farthest, darkest corner of the basement. As the music builds toward a crescendo and you just know a monster is going to burst forth at any moment … someone's cell phone goes off, repeatedly playing the opening bars of that pop song you can never get out of your head no matter how hard you try.

From this moment forward, regardless of how gripped you've been by the movie, it will be difficult to get back into it in the same way.

Now let's watch another movie together. This is a movie about you. It's filled with problems and obstacles and triumphs and tragedies. It's a movie where you see yourself failing to achieve what you want to achieve, being dragged down again and again by your tragic personal history, or succeeding against the odds and triumphing in the end. It's a movie about how difficult it is to find true love, or how lucky you are to have found it for yourself, how men and women are sinners or saints, and how people always mean well or stab you in the back every time. Whether you're stuck in a cubicle or living it large in a corner office, working from home or not working at all, this is the movie of your life – for better, for worse, for richer, for poorer, in sickness and in health.

This time, instead of waiting for a cell phone to start ringing, I'm going to ask you to turn your attention away from the screen and come with me up into the projection booth.

As we look out from the projection booth over the audience, we can see the screen of consciousness at the front of the theater. Whatever is happening on the screen is your experience of life. What's being projected onto that screen will appear real to you, even though at some level you know it's just a movie.

Each reel of film running in front of the projector is made up of your thoughts. If you have scary thoughts, you'll see scary things on the screen of your experience and experience scary feelings; if you're projecting romantic thoughts, you'll see romantic things on the screen and tend to feel romantic feelings in your heart. Comedies will usually make you laugh and tragedies make you cry – that's just the way things work.

Why does all this matter? Because even if you're watching a film you really don't enjoy, you're unlikely to try to change it by getting into a prolonged debate with the characters on the screen about what they're up to. And if you do, you probably don't expect them to respond in turn.

But when it comes to the movie of our lives, the first place most of us go to change things is right up to the screen. We spend all our time and money and energy trying to change our experience on the outside, not realizing that the whole thing is being projected from the inside out.

Or let's change the metaphor from movies to dreams. As Syd Banks repeatedly said, 'Life is a divine dream, suspended between the boundaries of time, space and matter.' So what do we do when the dream of life starts to seem like a nightmare? Can we change the dream at will? How do we master the art of dreaming?

EXPLORING THE VERTICAL DIMENSION OF LIFE

In the introduction to this book, I talked about the difference between the horizontal and vertical dimensions of life. The horizontal dimension represents what is sometimes called 'the dash' – the distance traveled and milestones passed between birth and death. The vertical dimension, on the other hand, represents our *relationship* with that journey.

To better understand the difference between these two dimensions, let me share a real-life case study that walked into my office not long ago. A friend of my daughter had just discovered (via text message) that she was not being accepted into the advanced performance group at her dance company. Resplendent in anger and frustration, she laid out the insensitivities, biases, and incompetences on the part of the decision-making panel that had led to her rejection and a detailed list of possible actions to get the decision reversed. She then asked me for help in three areas:

1. A crash course in effective negotiation and influence strategies to assist her in persuading the panel of their error.

2. Designing a back-up plan for what to do if she was unsuccessful in her attempts, including a potential smear

campaign against the relevant parties so that they would lose their jobs and more sensible and appropriately skilled people would be able to review and assess her potential.

3. Brainstorming possible alternative career options if this proved to be indicative of the realities of the industry to which she was committing her life.

Now, each one of these interventions would have made perfect sense in the horizontal dimension, where our primary goal is to improve our experience of life by changing our circumstances in a particular way. But in the vertical dimension, our primary goal is to transform our relationship with circumstances. We do this by gaining a deeper, more insightful understanding of what's really going on *behind* our experience of life. While that understanding inevitably leads to clearer thinking, better decisions, and a higher quality of life, it does so indirectly and in ways that are often surprising.

One of the things we'll talk about in our fifth session together is that when you're drowning in negative emotion, it's a terrible time to trust your thinking. So I counseled my young friend patience in the short term, promising that if she came back later that afternoon, we could revisit her plan after she had allowed herself a bit of time to regain her bearings and take a look at things with fresh eyes.

While she was initially frustrated by my 'unwillingness to help,' a few hours later she returned to tell me, quite sheepishly, that the text message turned out to have been a ruse – a misguided attempt on the part of a well-meaning friend to make her think she hadn't made it so that she'd be all the more delighted the next day when the head of the company planned to announce her successful 'promotion' in front of all of her peers.

On reflection, the head of the company was actually 'a very good judge of talent and a very nice person,' dance was 'the only thing in the world she wanted to pursue,' and the idea of sitting down to study negotiation, persuasion, and influence was 'kind of boring' and would I mind terribly if we left it to another time?

Now, it's easy to dismiss this story as the result of an artistic temperament and to point out that your problems are real and not due to this kind of comedy of errors. But in my experience, our problems are always the result of a simple yet fundamental misunderstanding:

> We think we're experiencing
> reality, but we're actually
> experiencing our thinking.

In other words, we think we have a reality problem, when in reality we have a thinking problem. And the more time we spend trying to 'improve reality,' the more real our thinking appears to us. This is the ultimate dilemma of the horizontal dimension – no matter how much time and energy we put into tuning up the engine of an imaginary car, it's still not going to get us where we really want to go.

By way of contrast, in the vertical dimension we recognize that we are always already exactly where we need to be. Wellbeing is right here, right now, and there is nothing we need to do, achieve, or change in order to be happy and at peace in this moment.

The more deeply we understand the nature of Thought, the more we see the world around us with clarity and insight. And the more we experience the deeper feelings that are our birthright, the more apparent it becomes that many of our attempts to improve our lot in life in the horizontal dimension are little more than a stressful distraction.

Of course, we can no more live purely in the vertical dimension than we can in the horizontal. Life seems designed to be experienced in 3D, and even though we may know at some level it's just a trick of perception that makes it appear this way, we will still get caught up and at times overwhelmed by the illusion.

But if we can let go of even a little bit of the compulsion to fix our problems and improve our lot, we'll notice that the edges of the world get a bit softer and life seems a whole lot less frightening. Because there's less 'reality' to fix, there's a lot less to do and a lot more time to do it in. Which means that when we find a circumstance we actually do want to change or create in the world, we have all the energy and resources we need to succeed.

The only thing you need to remember is this:

It's all made up, and it's all okay.

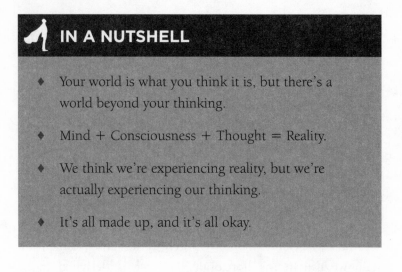

IN A NUTSHELL

♦ Your world is what you think it is, but there's a world beyond your thinking.

♦ Mind + Consciousness + Thought = Reality.

♦ We think we're experiencing reality, but we're actually experiencing our thinking.

♦ It's all made up, and it's all okay.

If you like, you can take some time to just sit with what we've been discussing before moving on. Go back through this session as often as you like, check it out in your experience, and let it settle into your bones. When you're ready, we'll begin our next session together by exploring who you are, what happiness is, and where it really comes from...

Session Two

YOU WERE
BORN HAPPY

*'The fact that millions of people share
the same forms of mental pathology
does not make these people sane.'*

Erich Fromm

AN OLD SIOUX LEGEND

In ancient times, the Creator wanted to hide something from the humans until they were ready to see it. He gathered all the other creatures of creation to ask for their advice.

The eagle said, 'Give it to me and I will take it to the highest mountain in all the land,' but the Creator said, 'No, one day they will conquer the mountain and find it.'

The salmon said, 'Leave it with me and I will hide it at the very bottom of the ocean,' but the Creator said, 'No, for humans are explorers at heart, and one day they will go there too.'

The buffalo said, 'I will take it and bury it in the very heart of the Great Plains,' but the Creator said, 'No, for one day even the skin of the Earth will be ripped open, and they will find it there.'

The creatures of creation were stumped, but then an old blind mole spoke up. 'Why don't you put it inside them? That's the very last place they'll look.'

The Creator said, 'It is done.'

HOW TO BE MORE OF WHO YOU ALREADY ARE

Recently, a woman whose thoughts were in a terrible spin called in to my radio show. She was worried about everything and trying to solve all her problems at once.

I interrupted her litany of woes and asked her what I'm sure she thought was a complete non-sequitur. 'If you had a bowl of murky water and you wanted to make that water clear,' I said, 'what would you do?'

She thought for a moment and then suggested boiling it.

I laughed because I recognized that this was exactly what she was doing with her own thoughts. She was attempting to gain clarity by trying harder than ever to figure everything out. As a strategy, this is like increasing traffic to reduce pollution, turning up the volume to drown out the noise, or attempting to bomb your way to a peaceful resolution. It's not that these strategies have never been attempted; it's just that they hardly ever work.

If you want to make murky water clear, you have to leave it alone long enough for the murk to settle. The reason this works is because the nature of water is clear. The nature of the mind is clear, too, and the nature of a human being is well.

THE SOURCE OF WELLBEING

People often live as though their experience of life takes place on a continuum ranging from misery to joy.

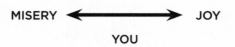

MISERY   ⟵⟶   JOY

YOU

The game of life then becomes about figuring out how to spend more time at the happy end of the continuum and less time at the miserable end.

At one level of understanding, this path toward greater happiness seems to be marked by having the right stuff – plenty of money, a good job, a great relationship, and a nice home. But we also recognize that there are any number of people who have all those things but are still pretty miserable inside themselves. So we begin to look more deeply and conclude that it's not our *stuff* that makes us happy or unhappy, but our *actions*. Do the right thing and you'll feel good about yourself; do the wrong thing and your conscience will haunt you until the end of time.

The problem with this is that most of us have noticed that as often as not, good things happen to bad people, and bad things happen to good people. And although we may think that 'doing the right thing' should be its own reward, life viewed from this level doesn't seem remotely fair.

It's thoughts like this that lead us in a more internal direction in our pursuit of happiness and wellbeing, and we often conclude that it's not what happens that determines our experience, but what we think about what happens. So we begin experimenting with things like affirmations and positive thinking, sure that if we could just control the flow of thoughts through our own brain, we'd have the key to lifelong happiness.

A lot of people get stuck on this idea because of one simple, innocent misunderstanding – they attribute their inability to think only positive thoughts to a lack of skill or effort on their part instead of recognizing that the theory itself is based on an incorrect premise: the idea that you can actually control which thoughts come into your head.

Here's a quick thought experiment: close your eyes and notice all the thoughts that come into your head in the next 60 seconds. I'll join you…

I noticed:

♦   rabbits

♦   sports cars

♦   liniment oil

♦   baseball

♦   the relative merits of killing a fly buzzing around my head

♦   sex, quickly followed by the thought that I can't mention that because it's such a cliché

♦   rabbits again

Now I don't know about you, but I'm pretty sure I didn't choose any of those thoughts. Which is what brings us to what seems like a real sticking point. As one of my clients once put it, 'If happiness doesn't come from what I have or what I do, and I can't choose my thoughts, doesn't that leave me kind of screwed?'

That's certainly the conclusion some people come to. They decide that happiness is completely outside their control, and they give up on the pursuit. Often they actually begin to feel better when they stop trying so hard to be happy, which leads them to another false conclusion: that happiness is something that can only be pursued indirectly. (The reason why that's a false conclusion is because it's based on the notion that happiness is a 'thing' – something we can have or not have, pursue directly or indirectly, get and/or if we're not careful, lose.)

Some people, in their pursuit of connection and wellbeing, or, as we're calling it, 'happiness,' decide that since they can't control which thoughts come into their heads, the thing to do is to try to stop thinking altogether. For reasons you'll understand in a few minutes, this seems to work, leading them into a complex set of routines, prayer, meditation practices, and a variety of other disciplines, all designed to at least temporarily stop thought. Since feelings of peace and wellbeing often follow these practices, the practices themselves appear to be the means to a happy end. But the problem with all of them is that they take practice – and while that may seem a small price to pay for such a precious jewel, the vast majority of people are unwilling or unable to put in 20 years of daily meditation for 20 minutes of daily bliss.

So let's take another look at our fundamental premise:

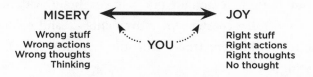

47

The one thing inherent in all these notions is the idea that misery and joy are somehow things that are outside us, and that we need to do things (or stop doing things) in order to get them. But here's another way of looking at it, one that stands our usual notions of where to go to find wellbeing on their head:

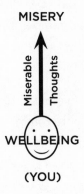

MISERY

Miserable Thoughts

WELLBEING

(YOU)

A quick look into a baby's eyes will reveal that we're born at peace – in tune with the infinite, in touch with our bliss, resting in the well of our being. But even when we're a baby, our very human needs from time to time interfere with our connection to this innate wellbeing. We experience physical discomfort, and because we don't yet understand the source of that discomfort, we do the best we know how to do – we scream bloody murder! Then, to our delight and amazement, someone comes and 'makes it better' – they feed our hunger, dry our bottom, entertain our nascent brain with funny noises and roller-coaster-type movements ... and before we know it, we're nestled back into the bosom of our innate wellbeing.

Over time, it's the most natural thing in the world for us to begin to connect and even attribute that return to wellbeing to the people or activities that seem to be causing it – we're okay because Mommy loves us; we're okay because Daddy protects us; we're okay because the people around us, for the most part, appear to have our wellbeing at heart. And then one day we do something in our innocence and joy that Mommy or Daddy doesn't like – we splash paint on a wall or cry when Daddy is tired – and suddenly the ocean of love we're used to swimming in is filled with sharks and other monsters too horrible to mention. Before long, we've bought into the myth that love and wellbeing exist outside us, and the need for a personality is born.

But wellbeing – happiness, contentment, love, peace, spirit – is our essential nature. So all our attempts to capture these feelings from out in the world, no matter how well intended and practically followed, are doomed to fail. Not because happiness and wellbeing are unattainable, but simply because it's impossible to find what has never been lost.

This leads us to our second secret:

> **Wellbeing is not the fruit of something
> you do; it's the essence of who you are.
> There is nothing you need to change, do,
> be, or have in order to be happy.**

The reason why this understanding of the source of wellbeing is so significant is that so much of our energy and time is squandered in pursuing goals and projects and financial incentives and relationships that we believe will make us happy. And so much of the stress and strain we experience in our lives is brought on by our misguided attempt to make ourselves feel better by having, doing, or achieving the 'right' things.

Simply put, what we attribute our good feelings to will determine what we do and where we go to get more of them.

♦ If I think my wellbeing comes from being around a particular person, I'll do all sorts of things I wouldn't otherwise do and put up with all sorts of things I wouldn't otherwise put up with in order to keep that person around.

♦ If I think my wellbeing comes from my work or my income, then I'll overinvest in my job and even be willing to ignore my common sense and wisdom in order to preserve or enhance it.

♦ If I think my wellbeing comes from a food or drug, I'll do whatever it takes to get hold of that food or drug the next time I'm feeling in need of another 'hit' of good feelings.

Because of the nature of Thought, whatever we continue to think will continue to appear to be real. Our world is what we think it is, and when we think that any of these things will make us happier, they will – at least for a time.

But when we begin to understand that wellbeing is our nature, not a goal to be pursued, we'll quickly realize that the moment the murk settles and our head clears, Consciousness itself will wake us back up to who and what we really are.

Exploring our deeper nature is a lifetime pursuit and the endgame of a number of spiritual traditions and practices. But most of us get so caught up in the drama of our personalities that we miss out on the joy and wisdom that are an ever-deepening presence at the level of our essential nature.

The Birth of a Personality

Some years ago, I watched the somewhat laughable 1950s romantic drama *Scaramouche* starring Stewart Granger and Janet Leigh. In the movie, a hideously scarred actor has been making his living playing a masked romantic clown by the name of Scaramouche. At some point, unbeknownst to the local police, his mask is taken over by a handsome political radical played by Granger.

Granger is able to function right under the noses of the local police because they believe they know all about the hideous creature that lives beneath the mask. In the same way, most of us have spent so long pretending to be whatever it is we're pretending to be that any pretense of living from our true selves is long gone. We begin to make up a new story, one based on our underlying awareness that we're not who we appear to be – that at any moment, we'll be unmasked and found out as the phonies and frauds that we are. The more energy we put into developing our mask, the more convinced we become that we really need one.

Unlike our true nature, which is something we're all born with, our personalities are conditioned and maintained throughout our lives. At first, they develop as a kind of unconscious reaction to what is going on in the world around us.

To better understand this, imagine yourself inside a 'motel womb.' You've been there for around nine months, so you're feeling completely at home, although lately things have been a bit cramped. You're relaxing on your heated waterbed, snacking on placenta-flavored potato chips, minding your own business, when all of a sudden – boom! – you feel an earthquake start to shake the bed. Before you know it, you're being pushed out through the door by an unseen force with the intensity of a tornado. You stumble out into blinding light, get smacked on the behind by a masked giant, and begin to scream.

It's hardly surprising at this point that you feel disoriented, disconnected, and in danger. That initial experience of danger is so profound that we begin to crave security – the knowledge that not only are we safe now, but that we'll always be safe. Whenever we feel unsafe, we seek to control our environment, and particularly the people around us, in order to return to safety. Now, some of these people will allow us a degree of control over them through the intensity of our feelings, especially if, through our anger or sadness or fear, we're able to stimulate their own insecure thinking and desire to feel safe. But sooner or later we come to the realization that we can't control everyone.

However, even if we can't control people, we soon work out that we can still feel safe around them.

How?

Well, it turns out that if people approve of what we're doing, they won't hurt us (most of the time). So we learn to be 'nice' and to do as we're told so that they approve of us and we get to stay safe – at least for as long as they keep approving of us.

In doing so, we begin to develop a personality – an act – that will fool all those scary giants out there into believing that we're actually the way they want us to be. The problem comes when we forget that it's just an act – when we start to believe that we actually are who we've been pretending to be.

As a friend of mine once put it, we're like diamonds who have spent so much time applying layer upon layer of nail polish to appear beautiful to the world that we begin to believe we must be covered in horse crap.

There's a lot of well-intended advice in the world focused on finding better ways to apply the nail polish. Most therapy is spent digging through the horse crap. But the 'supercoach approach' is to go inside and uncover the diamond within.

Do You Really Need to Work on Your Self-Worth?

Jeremy had joined a multi-level marketing company and hired me to help him boost his self-worth. He'd heard a motivational speaker talking about the importance of self-image and self-esteem in creating success and had decided that what was holding him back was his low opinion of himself.

In our first session together, I asked him how he knew that low self-worth was what was holding him back.

He looked shocked. 'Don't you need high self-worth to succeed?'

Having worked with some of the most successful people in Hollywood, the majority of whom had the self-esteem of a gnat, I knew that most of what people call 'self-worth' is actually a reflection of Thought taking form in the moment, and goes up and down on a thought-by-thought basis.

I then told Jeremy the story of when my son, Oliver, was first learning to play baseball. A few weeks into the season, he came to me and said, 'Daddy, I want to quit – I don't want to play anymore.' When I asked him why, he shocked me by saying, 'Because I'm crap at baseball.'

Now, if I'd really thought that self-image and self-esteem were the keys to success, I would have given him the 'Go get 'em, tiger' speech. I would have talked to him about how he needed to 'believe to achieve' and 'whether you think you can or you can't, you're right.'

But when he said to me, 'I'm crap at baseball,' I said to him, 'Yes, you are. But here's the question: do you want to get good at it?'

Well, his little eyes lit up. It had never occurred to him that being good at baseball was something you could learn, not something you were born able to do.

I said to him, 'Here's how we do it. Every day you're gonna throw me 50 throws and I'm going to throw you 50, and we're going to take 50 swings, and I guarantee within a month you're going to be pretty good at this.'

And we did, and he was, and strangely enough, he started liking it a whole lot more as well.

The reason self-worth is so important, or so the experts tell us, is that we'll inevitably live up or down to our self-image – that is, we'll become more and more like the person we think (or are afraid) we really are. So if someone believes or 'sees themselves' as shy, they'll tend to behave shyly; if they see themselves as confident, they'll tend to behave in a more confident manner.

This leads to a host of Level I and Level II interventions. At Level I, we use our physiology to create a greater sense of confidence by standing up straight, putting our shoulders back, and looking people straight in the eye. We might back this up with both affirmations ('I am confident, I *am* confident, I am *confident!*') and affirmative actions of the 'feel the fear and do it anyway' variety.

At Level II, we go to work on the self-image directly. We use hypnosis, relaxation, and guided visualization to change the pictures we have of ourselves in our mind. We run movies of our past successes and condition ourselves over 21 days or 30 days or however long we think it will take for us to begin to see ourselves in a new light.

Now, it's important to point out that this may well have an impact on the way we see ourselves. But even if I'd done all that with Oliver, he would still have been crap at baseball – he would just have *thought* he was good at it.

This is echoed by a series of global studies (for a comprehensive overview see www.michaelneill.org/supercoach) on the relationship between self-esteem and math ability in middle-school students. Of the 10 countries with the highest level of student confidence, only Israel and the United States scored higher than average on the international test, and their scores were far below those of the much less confident students in Japan, Korea, Hong Kong, and Taiwan.

When I suggested to Jeremy that rather than work on his confidence, self-image, or even self-esteem, he should work on his business and the creative art of selling, he seemed a bit disappointed. But I then talked with him about the true source of self-worth: his own innate wellbeing. I pointed out that when we take our focus off creating a more beautiful mask and put it on uncovering our true nature, we discover that underneath the mask and underneath all the thoughts about what's wrong with us is something really rather wonderful.

In the end, Jeremy decided that he would rather spend his time being happy and going for what he wanted than going for what he wanted in the hope that it would one day make him happy. In less than a year of connecting with the diamond of his essence, he had become a 'diamond' in his network as well.

Supercoaching Tip
Take a Self-Improvement Vacation

1. Take a week off from working on yourself in any way. Don't try to change, improve, or fix yourself – just enjoy hanging out with your work, your hobbies, and your loved ones.

2. If you can't bring yourself to take the whole week off, take a few days off.

3. If you can't bring yourself to take a few days off, just take one.

4. If you can't even take one day off from putting nail polish on your diamond, repeat step one.

IN A NUTSHELL

♦   Wellbeing is not the fruit of something you do; it's the essence of who you are.

♦   There is nothing you need to change, do, be, or have in order to be happy.

♦   You are a diamond, buried in horse crap, coated in nail polish.

♦   If you want to get better at something, work on your craft, not on yourself.

Hopefully, you're beginning to get a feel for how different life can be as you start waking up to the thought-created nature of your experience and rest in the simple feeling of being who you already are.

In our next session, we'll take a fresh look at goals and goal-setting. Until then, have fun, learn heaps, and enjoy the rest...

A WHOLE NEW WAY OF THINKING ABOUT GOALS

*'The good life begins when you
stop wanting a better one.'*

Nkosiphambili E. Molapis

'WHY DOES A BIRD SING?'

A teacher who had received much acclaim for his insights and discourses into the nature of the universe was asked by one of his students what difference he hoped to make in the world through his teaching.

After a few moments' thought, the teacher replied that he had no such hopes.

'Those who can truly hear what I have to say don't really need me to say it; those who can't hear could listen until I was hoarse without changing in the slightest.'

The student was confused.

'But if you can't make a difference, why do you teach at all?'

The teacher smiled.

'Why does a bird sing?'

A GREAT BIG GAME OF FETCH

When my kids were young we had two dogs, Mishka and Abby, who had very different personalities. Mishka was bored unless engaged in her favorite game, which, as you might imagine for a dog, was 'fetch.' You would take her bone and throw it as far as you could, and she would chase it as fast as she could. Then she would bring it back to you and ask (well, beg) you to throw it again. She wanted to play fetch continually, and I occasionally speculated that if I let her, she would keep chasing that bone right up to the point where she collapsed of physical exhaustion.

I called Mishka a 'goal dog,' because her behavior was similar to what I saw in compulsive goal-setters. They continually set goals in every area of their lives, driving themselves forward relentlessly toward the ever-receding target of 'making it.' They rarely stop to consider what they would do if they did make it, and those who do succeed (at least by society's standards) often find themselves bored and empty until they throw themselves back into the fray.

Essentially, compulsive goal-setting is like playing a game of fetch with yourself – you throw the bones as far as you can (set the biggest goals you can imagine), and then chase after them with hyper-focused attention and continual action. The problem comes when your happiness and self-worth are attached to the bones.

For most compulsive goal-setters, their sense of wellbeing comes from how well they think they're doing. And since they're constantly raising the bar on what 'success' and 'making it' mean, they're never doing well enough to feel happy and worthwhile. There's always more action to be taken and more targets to be reached, so there's never a sense of being content right where they are now. And, as is too often the case, if they let themselves, they keep chasing those goals right up to the point where they collapse of physical exhaustion, mental burnout, or ill health.

My other dog, Abby, was more of what I called a 'river dog.' I called her that based on the writing of motivational speaker Earl Nightingale (co-founder of Nightingale-Conant), who described 'river people' as being those who 'are happiest and most alive when they're in the river – in whatever business or career or profession it happens to be. And success comes to such people as inevitably as a sunrise. In fact, they are successes the moment they find their great field of interest; the worldly trappings of success will always come in time.'

Abby loved the park, and she loved the house. She loved going for a run with my son, but she seemed equally happy and content to hang out on the sofa with our cats. In fact, wherever Abby was, she threw herself into the mix without ever seeming to need things to be a certain way.

Bizarrely, the one game Abby would almost never play was fetch. You could throw her bone as often as you liked, but unless you went and got it yourself, it would never be seen again.

When it comes to us human beings, I think of these two approaches to life as being less about personality types than levels of understanding. If we think our wellbeing is dependent on circumstances, 'there' will always look better than here and we'll be on a constant journey toward ever greener shades of grass. If we know our wellbeing is innate, we're far less likely to turn our 'bone of happiness' into a bone of contention and throw it off into some imaginary future, and far more likely to enjoy gnawing on it right here, right now.

Here's the third secret:

> There's nowhere for you to get
> to – you're already here.

Of course, just because there's nowhere to get to doesn't mean you'll no longer travel – just that you'll no longer do so in order to get somewhere that's better than right where you're sitting now. It doesn't mean that you can't upgrade your car, your job, your finances, or even your relationship. It just means that if you do, it will be because you *want* to, not because you think you *have* to or you *should*.

This idea can be disturbing at first to people who feel that 'the next big thing' is continually just around the corner. But if they sit with it, most feel their shoulders begin to relax as their experience of the present moment deepens.

For instance, I worked with an executive named John who adamantly refuted the idea that there was no inherent goal in life. Rather than get into an argument with him, I showed him a cartoon I'd found in a magazine of a business executive in a suit running on a treadmill with a dollar bill attached to his forehead, just out of reach.

John didn't find it remotely funny, but I could tell that it triggered some sort of insight inside him. Before our next session, he sent me this quote attributed to the comedienne Lily Tomlin:

> *The trouble with the rat race is that even if you win, you're still a rat.*

HOW TO GET WHAT YOU WANT

In our culture, there are essentially three main ways people have learned to go for and get what they want...

The School of Acquisition

The school of acquisition has been the dominant one in Western culture for many years, and its teachings can be summed up in a sentence: 'If you want it, go and get it!'

From the ancient Mongol hordes to the modern titans of business and industry, our society tends to reward and hold up as heroes those men and women who have gone after what they wanted with enthusiasm and passion. (If they have trampled a few people on the way to the top ... well, it's unfortunate, of course, but that's just collateral damage.)

In the acquisition model of the world, the stuff of life is out there somewhere, and your job is to go and get it. Acquisition-based thinkers often see life as a case of the 'haves' versus the 'have-nots,' and shift between the roles of hero and victim in a 'dog eat dog' world.

On the plus side, graduates of the school of acquisition have helped create ancient and modern empires and contributed to tremendous advances in science, medicine, and business; on the minus side, they have contributed to a world culture where the strong tend to look down on the weak and wonder why they don't just get off their lazy behinds, try harder, and 'go and get it' for themselves.

The School of Attraction

While the school of acquisition has been in full session for the past 2,500 years or so, the school of attraction has been quietly holding classes in hidden caves and New Thought churches, its teachings disseminated through secret texts, biblical parables, and New Age gurus. Many of the great men and women throughout history, from ancient religious icons to Renaissance men like Leonardo da Vinci and Sir Isaac Newton, are known to have studied the ancient texts of this school.

The school of attraction teaches:

Like attracts like. Thoughts become things.

and:

You become what you think about.

These 'secret' teachings and principles have often been suppressed by the ruling elite, or so the story goes, because they place power within each individual, although the true source of that power is often attributed to God or a benevolent vibratory universe.

So now that this 'secret' teaching is no longer a secret, why isn't everybody living the life of their dreams?

A woman who wanted to hire me as her coach told me that she had been deeply inspired by what she had been reading about the law of attraction. She had already applied the teachings to attract a new job, a great apartment, and a boyfriend who, in her words, 'actually seems to really like me.'

When I asked her what she hoped to get out of our work together, she was quiet for a few moments before somewhat shyly telling me, 'I'm terrified that it will stop working, and I'll go back to being miserable and alone.'

Here's the problem: people are attempting to use the law of attraction as a new set of tools for acquisition.

Instead of actually shifting the basis of their approach to life to one of planting seeds of kindness, beauty, and love, and reaping the harvest of a bountiful life, people are attempting to get a better parking space (or indeed a better car, boyfriend, or bank balance) by 'thinking the right thoughts.'

The source of the problem lies in the reason people want the car, boyfriend, or bank balance in the first place – because they believe having what they want will make them happy. But a closer look at the teachings of the school of attraction reveals that it works the other way around: it is the energy of happiness that attracts the good things into our lives.

Does the law of attraction really work? In my experience, absolutely. But if you try to use it to manipulate the universe into giving you what you think you need in order to be happy, you're as likely to manifest frustration and self-doubt as that shiny new husband or loving automobile.

This leads us to a third way of thinking about getting what we want in our lives...

The School of Creation

When I first ask people what they want, they generally go up into their heads to order off an invisible menu of possibilities that have been programmed and conditioned into their brains throughout their lives. For many of us, that menu is so limited that 'Nothing seems to inspire me' is a common complaint. We don't know what we really want, so we go for the best thing we can find, assuming that something will be better than nothing but ultimately feeling uncreative, unsatisfied, and unfulfilled by what we get.

This is one of the reasons why even a traditional coach can be such a huge help in moving forward – the coach generally has access to a larger menu with more choices, consequently opening up new possibilities in the minds of their clients.

But while asking 'What do you want?' with intention and awareness can certainly get at the real desires lurking underneath the straitjacket of societal acceptability, a question that seems to evoke a different quality of answer is this:

What would you love to create?

When we come to the table as creators, we're no longer limited by whatever happens to be on the menu, because we know we can always go into the kitchen and cook up something wonderful of our own.

And what if, instead of seeing ourselves at a cosmic restaurant, we viewed our lives as a blank canvas, a musical score waiting to be written, or even a raw, unformed lump of clay? We would then be free to be about creating absolutely anything – and if we didn't like what we'd created so far, we could always throw it away and start again. Then the natural artistry we were born with would have the space to come out and play, and our circumstances would stop being 'good' or 'bad,' or 'right' or 'wrong,' but simply be the raw materials for our next creation.

The reality is, your essential nature is infinitely creative. And when you take the best of what's inside you and use it to create cool things in the world, concepts like success, abundance, and a meaningful legacy stop appearing to be goals to be pursued and instead become the natural fruits of your creative nature.

When you set out in a direction but don't wind up with what you wanted to create, it's either because you haven't yet found a way or it's just taking more time than you wanted it to. No blame, no fault, no problem.

And when creating what you want stops being about you and becomes about what you actually want to create, the whole game gets a whole lot easier.

A QUESTION OF CONTROL

One of the questions I will often ask my goal-seeking clients is this:

*On a scale from 0 percent to 100 percent, how much say
do you think you have in how things turn out?*

While the answers vary greatly, most people wind up seeing
that they're less in control than they thought, but more in
control than they feared. Or as I like to put it:

It's not up to you — but it's not not up to you.

And that leads to an interesting question:

How do we create in a world where we are not in control?

If we think we are the predominant creative force in the
universe, the power of our will is the force we must harness to
create what we want to see in the world. But if the predominant
creative force in the universe is the universe itself, then it is
in our relationship with that force that we find the power to
influence creation.

In that sense, all acts of initiative and creation are actually
co-creations. And whether 'God is our co-pilot' or we are the
co-pilot to the gods, understanding that it's not up to us but
it's not *not* up to us is a pivotal piece of the puzzle.

In this co-created universe, clarity of intention becomes our
primary tool in the game of creation. Simply put, when we're
really clear about what we're up to, the universe has a way
of moving the pieces around behind the scenes to make the
impossible possible.

But what's to stop us from attempting to use intention as a tool
of volition?

Nothing but the fact that it doesn't seem to work anywhere near as well. Telling yourself that you intend to create something you don't really want to create is as ineffective and self-defeating as attempting to commit to it and use discipline and willpower to follow through and make things happen. In this sense, intention is something we uncover, not something we create.

The power of intention is already at work in the daily creation of your life. It's just that much of that intention is unconscious and often conflicting. For example, many years ago one of my coaches pointed out to me that I had an apparently unconscious intention to fly under the radar. She pointed to the years of coaching and teaching I had managed to do with thousands of people without anyone who hadn't worked with me directly having any idea of who I was.

Attempting to assert my will over the situation, I declared my intention to fly 'over the radar,' not quite seeing that that would still be off the radar of the vast majority of humanity. So, not knowing what to do, I did what I know to do when I don't know what to do: I just sat with it. All sorts of thoughts came to light, ranging from *If I become known, people will see that I'm a fraud* to *If I become famous, I'll wind up doing drugs and cheating on my wife.*

Then one day, quite by chance, I was sitting in my car outside a friend's apartment in Hollywood when a beautiful woman started walking down the street toward me stripping off her clothes. When my lower jaw rehinged and I was able to regain my senses, I realized I was in the midst of a guerilla-style porno shoot, and that the woman wasn't actually walking toward me, she was walking towards a camera crew that was standing in the middle of the street behind where I was parked.

Something about the absurdity of the situation popped me out of my habitual thinking, and I realized two things in quick succession. First, I don't particularly enjoy drugs and I don't ever want to cheat on my wife. Second, being at least willing to become better known was an essential part of any business growth strategy I could think of.

At that moment, my thinking clarified itself and becoming more of a public figure went from a 'good idea/bad idea' conundrum to a clear, clean, and simple intention. Within a week, I had received and accepted a teaching offer that put me in front of tens of thousands of people over the next few years and led directly to my first book deal.

Coincidence? Yes, but as we'll explore in a moment, coincidences and 'happy accidents' are reliable occurrences on the journey to success.

Time to Reflect

- Have a look for yourself and see where in your life you are trying to make things happen through force of will as opposed to harnessing (or being harnessed by) the inner creative forces of innate intelligence and unlimited thought.

- If your life as it is today were a product of your intentions, conscious and unconscious, what intentions would be revealed?

Balancing Effort and Grace

When my daughter Maisy won first place in a dance competition and the scholarship and meeting with an agent that came with it, my first thought was: *Who knew that putting in four to six hours a day six days a week for years would pay off?*

While I'm obviously immensely proud of her natural ability (inherited, I am obliged to point out, from her mother), I know that unnurtured talent and a $5 bill will get you a grande latte at Starbucks and very little else. I also know that putting in the hours doesn't always pay off – otherwise everyone who works long enough and hard enough would play for their favorite sports team, win Olympic gold, run a successful company, and change the world.

But the opposite *is* true – nobody who *doesn't* put in the hours succeeds at anything of note in any significant way.

Supercoaching Tip
Action Days

Sometimes all the psychological insight in the world won't get you unstuck or move you forward as quickly as simply taking action. That's why when my clients seem overly caught up in theories on why they're stuck, we book an 'action day.'

To create an action day for yourself:

1. Enlist the help of a buddy or coach. Every hour on the hour, phone in or message them to let them know what actions you intend to take in the next hour.

2. Then, no matter what else you might be up to, reach back out an hour later to let them know what you've done so far and what you've got planned for the next hour!

Since effort alone is not enough to guarantee success, we need to depend in equal measure on what might be called happy accidents, or grace. Fortunately, moments of grace are surprisingly dependable.

There are many ways of defining 'grace,' but perhaps my favorite in the context of creating is 'unearned rewards.' Grace is the inspired solution that arrives unbidden in the middle of the night, the celebrity you've never met who tweets about how great your product is to their millions of fans, the stranger you bump into in a coffee shop who is the perfect person to help you move your project forward.

Some people think of it in terms of synchronicity, others as luck, still others as a gift from God or the gods. In *Creating the Impossible*, I write about it like this:

> *If you take a fresh look at it, you'll see that a remarkable amount of success in the world comes down to people staying in the game long enough to 'get lucky.' Fortunately, the emergence of luck, grace, and synchronicity is a predictable part of the process.*
>
> *You can rest assured that when you show up to your life and start moving in a direction, the creative potential of the deeper Mind will show up with you. And you can have equal faith in the fact that if you keep moving in the*

direction of your goals and dreams, fresh possibilities and previously unseen opportunities will begin to emerge.

Here's a simple rule of thumb:

> As you begin moving in the direction of your dreams, the emergence of fresh new thinking and unexpected synchronicities (i.e. 'luck') is 100 percent reliable and 98 percent unpredictable.

Whether your missing ingredient is more hours than grace or vice versa can be difficult to self-diagnose. My guideline (based on purely experiential and anecdotal evidence) is that if you think that you're lazy and just need to work harder, you're probably already a workaholic; if you think you just need to 'let go and let God,' you probably need to get off the couch, put in more hours, and engage more fully with the task at hand.

Either way, if you're not creating the results you want to see in the world, chances are you're suffering from a deficit in at least one of these two areas.

So what's the solution?

To get more out of anything we do, we first need to put more of ourselves into it. What both makes us better at whatever it is we do and invites in more grace, luck, and synchronicity is to throw ourselves into it as though it were the most important job in the world, knowing full well that it probably isn't.

OBSTACLE OR EXCUSE?

When I was a child, my favorite sport to watch on TV (and on very special occasions in the stadium) was American football. I spent years playing in my backyard and the school playground, and then when I was 12, my parents finally let me sign up to play in a 'real' league. I was so excited that I couldn't wait to get into pads and transform myself into a pint-size replica of my gridiron heroes. However, the first day of practice was more like a military boot camp than my fantasies of football glory. If you've never thrown on the pads of a football uniform, the one thing you may not realize is how heavy they are, particularly when you're 12. In full uniform, we spent the practice doing push-ups and sit-ups and running so many sprints that several of us threw up in the grass by the side of the field.

Finally, at the end of that first practice, they set up a mini-game to let us show them what we had. Unfortunately for me, what I had left at that point wasn't really worth having. On the very first play from scrimmage, our quarterback threw the ball downfield in my general direction, only to have it intercepted right in front of me by one of the largest 12-year-olds I'd ever seen. Caught between my exhaustion, fear, and desire to prove my manhood, I gave chase and was actually closing in on him when one of the other team's players threw himself to the ground in front of me in a last-ditch attempt to trip me up. At that moment, time stood still. I realized I had a choice: to carry on the lung-burning, leg-aching pursuit of my prey or to let myself trip over this would-be blocker and finally get a rest.

In the years since that moment, I've found that the same kind of dilemma faces us nearly every day in the pursuit of our dreams. Things come up between us and our goals – something we don't yet know how to do, an unexpected bill, an overprotective gatekeeper, a child who doesn't sleep, or a spouse who somehow doesn't quite grasp the magnificence of our vision. What we do in those moments is ultimately what determines our destiny:

♦ If we treat whatever stands in our way as an *obstacle*, we can bring the full creative resources of our mind to bear on the situation and find ways to get over, around, or through it.

♦ If we use it as an *excuse*, we allow ourselves to be tripped up or otherwise stopped by it.

While I would love to say I leaped over that kid and carried on to save a touchdown, the truth is that I let my foot catch on his shoulder pad and tumbled to the ground. I thought I'd feel relief, but what I actually felt was embarrassment and shame.

Now, of course, I know there's no embarrassment in a 12-year-old taking himself 'out of the game' when he's exhausted and frightened. But I've also realized as an adult what a shame it is to allow an obstacle to become an excuse.

With that in mind, here's how simple going for what you want really is…

I'm writing this in my office. Let's say I want to walk outside to enjoy the California sunshine. Unless my legs suddenly give way or someone leaps out from behind my sofa and tackles me (a somewhat creepy, if extremely unlikely, possibility), I'm going to do it. In fact, short of an act of God or other unpredictable event, the only thing that could stop me from walking out the door would be some sort of obstacle. But if I really wanted to go outside, even that wouldn't really matter. I could use my creative genius to find a way over or around that obstacle.

Because when you really want something, the question isn't 'How will you get it?', it's 'What could possibly stop you?'

IN A NUTSHELL

♦ Obsessing about goals is like playing a game of fetch with yourself, using your happiness and self-worth as the bone.

♦ There's nowhere for you to get to – you're already *here*.

♦ It's not up to you, but it's not *not* up to you.

♦ Your essential nature is infinitely creative.

♦ To get more out of anything you do, you first need to put more of yourself into it.

You might want to take a break before moving on to the next session. You can stretch your legs, go for a walk, or just take some time to reflect on what you've been learning.

When you're ready, I'll see you there...

THE SIMPLE WAY TO MAKE DECISIONS

'You do not need to leave your room. Remain sitting at your table and listen. Do not even listen, simply wait. Do not even wait, be quite still and solitary. The world will freely offer itself to you to be unmasked. It has no choice. It will roll in ecstasy at your feet.'

Franz Kafka

THE LION AND THE FOX

A man was walking through the woods outside his home one day when he came across a hungry fox who seemed to be at death's door. Because he was a kind man, he thought to bring it some food, but before he could go back to his home, he heard a fearsome roar and hid behind a tree. In seconds, a mountain lion appeared, dragging the carcass of its freshly caught prey. The lion ate its fill and then wandered off, leaving the remains for the grateful fox.

The man was overwhelmed by this example of an abundant and benevolent universe and decided that he wouldn't return to his home or his job. Instead of working hard to provide for himself, he would follow the example of the fox and allow the universe to provide for him.

Needless to say, the fox wandered off, and as days turned to weeks, the man himself was hungry and at death's door. Despite his best efforts to retain his faith, he was becoming desperate. In a rare moment of inner quiet, he heard the still, small voice of his own wisdom: 'Why have you sought to emulate the fox instead of the lion?'

With that, the man returned home and ate his fill.

THE HEDGEHOG OF WISDOM

There is a line from the Greek poet Archilochus, which is generally translated as:

The fox knows many things, but the hedgehog knows one big thing.

While foxes might be cunning and able to devise hundreds of strategies for catching unsuspecting hedgehogs off guard and eating them for dinner, the hedgehog has only one defensive strategy: to curl up in a ball, spiky spines exposed, and wait until the fox (or other predator) gives up and goes away.

When it comes to making decisions, it seems to me that we have the same choice – to devise a thousand strategies for happiness and success, or to find one thing that really works and do it a thousand times.

The obvious question is this:

What's the one thing?

After nearly 30 years of coaching individuals and groups from nearly every walk of life, I can say with confidence that the people who do really well over time are often not the smartest, or best-read. They can be introvert or extrovert, seemingly self-assured or apparently neurotic and insecure. What they all have in common is that they have an unusually high degree of trust in their own sense of knowing, and a willingness to follow that sense right up to (and occasionally) over the edge of an apparent cliff if that's what it's guiding them to do. In other words, they have a deep relationship with and abiding faith in the wisdom within.

The fact that so many of us are so out of touch with that inner knowing is simply the result of a lifetime of 'fox training.' We've been innocently taught from the time we were born that the 'right' answers to our most important questions are out in the world around us, waiting to be found. So we search and we seek, and sure enough, there are thousands of people only too willing to share their best advice on how to find happiness, get everything we want, and outfox the other foxes to make our way in the world.

But meanwhile, the deeper mind – our inner knowing – is quietly whispering (and occasionally shouting) words of guidance, common sense, and direction in our ear. Sometimes that guidance takes the form of a 'no-brainer yes' or a 'no-brainer no' that makes decision-making effortless. More often than not, people experience it as a simple feeling of 'on track' or 'off track' that lets them know when to hold back and when to jump in with both feet, even if what they're jumping into seems way over their head at the time.

Ironically, the more we think about this inner knowing, the harder it is to feel, which is why most of us intuitively know that when the outcome seems to really matter, it's worthwhile pausing for breath and letting things settle before jumping ahead or pulling back.

But even when we lose our way, wisdom never leaves us. And when we know beyond a shadow of a doubt that our relationship with and faith in wisdom is all we need to live a life rich with meaning, purpose, and joy, it gets easier to hear its words. Then the fox of our cleverness doesn't need to be fed quite so often, and we begin to spend more and more of our time attending to the hedgehog of wisdom. The more we look within, the more we see; the more we see, the easier it is to do. And life gets better, moment by moment, one lovely day at a time.

This kind of common sense/innate wisdom approach to life is always available to us, but we spend so much of our time preoccupied, caught up in the whirlwind of our thoughts, that we don't notice it. And on the rare occasions when we do notice it, we often ignore it, hoping that our intellect can find an answer more in keeping with what we hope will turn out to be true.

I was explaining this idea in a meeting with a potential corporate client one day when one of the women in the room asked for an example. I went with the first one that popped into my head – that nearly every woman I've talked to who has come out the other side of a bad marriage has told me that she knew not to marry the guy at some point before getting far enough down the aisle to say 'I do.'

Before I could even finish my example, another of the women in the room burst into tears. It turned out that she was engaged to be married and was doing her best to ignore her wisdom because she didn't want to 'let anyone down.'

'Besides,' she asked me, 'how do I know whether that's some kind of inner wisdom or just fear?'

I was tempted to say, 'Ask your wisdom,' but I offered her the following guidelines...

♦ Wisdom is ever-present and always kind.

♦ Wisdom is sometimes soft but always clear.

♦ Wisdom has an obviousness to it when you hear it, even if it's completely invisible to you until you do

♦ Wisdom often comes disguised as 'common sense,' but in reality is extremely uncommon in usage.

Wisdom is right there inside you, just waiting for you to allow it to guide you. You need only be quiet and listen. When you relax into it, you'll almost always know what to do.

So why is decision-making so difficult for so many of us so much of the time?

Because we get caught up in a whirlwind of thinking that our future wellbeing is dependent on making the right decision now, and that in some way we could or should know in advance how things will turn out.

But what if you couldn't make a mistake because you can't know how things will turn out in advance and you can never know how things would have turned out if you'd done things differently? What if you are always doing the best you can, given the thinking you have that looks real to you?

The secret of effective decision-making is simply this:

There's no such thing as a 'decision' — you either know what to do or you don't.

Now at first glance that might just seem silly. What about all the decisions you've already made in your life about where to live, what profession to pursue, and which people to spend your time or even your life with?

Well, let me ask you a few questions:

♦ Did you *decide* which butt cheek to lean on right now, or which foot to have most of your weight on if you're standing up?

♦ Did you *decide* to take your last inhale, or when to exhale?

♦ What about the dozens of 'decisions' you need to make walking down the hallway at the office or down the aisles of a supermarket about whom to smile at and whom to ignore?

The fact is, we're making thousands of apparent 'decisions' every day without ever having to think about them, or in most cases even noticing them.

What we call 'decisions' are just those difficult-looking things we see when we drop out of the flow of our inner knowing and get caught back up in our habitual thinking.

As the secret in this session points out, in any given moment you either know what to do or you don't. When you do, life is easy; when you don't, life is easy too, unless you try to force yourself to answer a question you already know you don't know the answer to.

Supercoaching Tip
Follow the Flip

Here's one of my favorite ways of demonstrating to yourself that underneath the noise of your thinking, you already know what to do.

Think of a decision you'd like to make. It can be as seemingly inconsequential as where you'll have lunch today or as important as which person you'll marry or which career path you'll take. You're going to make this decision in the next 60 seconds.

Now, take out a coin and decide which of your options corresponds to 'heads' and which to 'tails.'

Ready?

In a moment, I'm going to ask you to flip the coin. If it's heads, you're going to take option A, and if it's tails, you're going to take option B. Before I do that, you have to promise to abide by the decision of the universe, as signified by the coin flip... (Just for fun, before we go any further, which way do you hope it lands, heads or tails?)

Okay, the moment of truth has arrived. Take a deep breath, flip the coin, and see which way your life has landed. (Quick question for you: How do you feel about that? Relieved? Excited? Disappointed?)

If you played along, you almost certainly experienced a physical, visceral response, seemingly to the flip of the coin but in actuality to the thinking that passed through your mind simultaneously. The way you felt before the coin was flipped and the way you felt afterward are fantastic access points to your inner wisdom.

Remember, *it doesn't matter which way the coin landed.* The feeling you had while it was in the air and the feeling after it landed will tell you all you need to know.

CONFABULATION AND PREDICTING THE FUTURE

The dictionary definition of the word 'confabulation' as a psychological term is: 'To fill in gaps in one's memory with fabrications that one believes to be facts.'

In other words, to 'confabulate' is to make up plausible-sounding reasons for often completely irrational decisions and actions. If you've ever watched a stage hypnosis show, you've probably seen the volunteers explaining quite rationally to the hypnotist why they were dancing like Mick Jagger or kissing a broomstick. That's confabulation in action!

Here's the problem with confabulation: when we confabulate 'very good reasons' why we behave in the ways that we do, we're setting ourselves up for a fall. That is because the decisions we make, actions we take, and moods we find ourselves in are part of the flow of thought. In other words, we do what we do because it 'seemed like a good idea at the time.' We know this at some level because if we regret it later, we say to ourselves,

'What was I thinking?'

In management consultant Frans Johansson's book *The Click Moment*, he makes a compelling case for the random factor and the role of unseen forces in almost every great human accomplishment. Through a series of disparate examples from the worlds of business, politics, music and more, he demonstrates the futility of attempting to predict the future success of any endeavor based on strategy, marketing, or even a track record of past results.

His conclusion is not that we should therefore give up on attempting to achieve, but that we should abandon excessive speculation about how likely something is to succeed as a decision-making criterion and adapt our execution strategy to take into account our extremely limited ability to predict the future.

As I thought about Johansson's thesis in my own business, it was easy to see how many projects I thought were destined for great success had floundered and how a few of my 'well, it's not going to work, but I really want to do it, so what the heck' projects had succeeded beyond my wildest imaginings. Yet what struck me most deeply in reflecting on this idea was that our inability to accurately predict the future, coupled with our blind faith that we *can* accurately predict the future, holds us back not only in the pursuit of success and happiness but also in tapping into the potential of the human mind.

Here are three kinds of prediction that most of us make on a regular basis, and a fourth kind that many of us are not even aware that we are making:

1. Predicting what will happen in the abstract

Imagine a fortune-teller comes up to you and with a bit of theatrical posturing, looks you in the eye and says: 'You seem to me like someone who has experienced a period of suffering in your life, but you have learned many important life lessons through that suffering and you are stronger now than you were before. And I can promise you that although there will be more suffering, you will also experience great good fortune!'

The reason you are likely to resonate with what they are saying is that it is filled with universal truths, including the facts that everyone suffers at some point in their lives, people are resilient, and sometimes things work out better than we expect them to.

Here are some more universal truths we can use to accurately predict the future *in the abstract*:

♦ Some things we attempt will work out and some won't.

♦ People we love will get ill and die. And at least one of those things will happen to us one day as well.

♦ Some things will take longer than we expect them to and some will happen more quickly.

♦ 'You miss 100 percent of the shots you never take' (ice hockey legend Wayne Gretsky).

2. Predicting what will happen in the specific

This is the realm that Frans Johansson speaks to in his book, and here are a couple of reasons why we can be seduced into thinking that the accuracy of our predictions is higher than it actually is:

♦ We don't take the self-fulfilling prophecy into account, so we don't see how our expectations shape our actions, and our actions (or lack thereof) influence our results.

♦ We don't take into account the nature of selective attention – the fact that we tend to see what we're looking for. If you've never done it, follow this link (www.michaelneill.org/supercoach) and count the number of times the white team passes the basketball.

3. Predicting our future experience

In Harvard professor Dan Gilbert's entertaining book *Stumbling on Happiness*, he details numerous studies demonstrating how ineffective we are at predicting which life experiences will lead to happiness and which to misery.

When you take into account the inside-out nature of experience – that we directly experience what's happening inside our head regardless of what may be happening outside it – it becomes easy to see why this is so.

Since we're designed to experience our thinking, that experience will inevitably change as our thoughts change. And our thoughts can change in a heartbeat.

Which points us to the fourth, slightly more insidious, type of prediction that we make…

4. Predicting our future thinking

What will you be thinking when you get to the end of this chapter?

We tend to believe that what we think now will be what we will think tomorrow and even for the rest of our life. So, when you're mad at your partner or colleague about something they've done, you assume that you'll still be mad about it in the same way the next time you see them. If you are open to it changing at all, you probably think it will change for the worse. After all, if it's this bad now, how bad will it be in six months, let alone in six years?

But have you ever noticed that there are some people you just can't stay mad at no matter what they've done?

This is because when we allow our thinking to flow naturally, we'll think ill of people in one moment and well of them in the next. And in our clarity of understanding, we know that this flow is part of the nature of thought and consequently don't get too caught up in believing that either of those judgments is inherently true.

The truth is, the nature of thought is to change. Whatever the world looks like to you now doesn't tell you *anything* about what the world will look like to you tomorrow. And since higher-order thinking is always available, it's not only possible but likely that today's crisis will be tomorrow's amusing or empowering anecdote.

When we're willing to simply trust ourselves and follow our inner knowing without confabulating a series of 'really good reasons' for what we've decided, we have a gentle rule of thumb for making decisions with impunity:

> **The number of reasons you have to do something is inversely proportional to how much you actually want to do it.**

Since our 'reasons' can't be trusted and we can't accurately predict the outcome of future actions, the only real basis for making a decision that doesn't 'decide itself' along the way is this:

Do you want to?

My perhaps somewhat obvious advice would be this:

If you want to, do; if you don't want to, don't.

Will this always lead to making the best possible decisions? No. But trying to always make the best possible decisions is part of what takes us out of the flow of our inner knowing and back up into the infinite noise-making device inside our head.

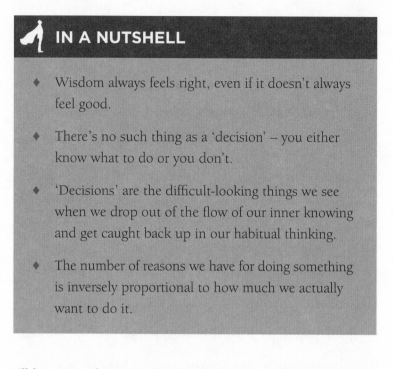

IN A NUTSHELL

- Wisdom always feels right, even if it doesn't always feel good.

- There's no such thing as a 'decision' – you either know what to do or you don't.

- 'Decisions' are the difficult-looking things we see when we drop out of the flow of our inner knowing and get caught back up in our habitual thinking.

- The number of reasons we have for doing something is inversely proportional to how much we actually want to do it.

I'll leave it with you to decide whether to move on to the next session right away or take a break to let what you've been learning soak in. When you're ready, we'll be exploring the role of emotions and feelings in helping us to wake up to our deeper potential and navigate the world with greater ease and grace…

Session Five

RAINY DAYS AND MONDAYS

'...life does not consist mainly – or even largely – of facts and happenings. It consists mainly of the storm of thoughts that is forever blowing through one's head.'

Mark Twain

THE ABBOT AND THE MONK

Many thousands of years ago, or so the story goes, the word of God was transcribed into written form. Because there were no computers, photocopiers, or even printing presses, monks would painstakingly copy each original text by hand. It could easily take a year to complete just one document.

A young monk who had abandoned the search for worldly pleasures wanted to see for himself the ancient texts and drink directly from the source of all wisdom. He volunteered to help copy them, but soon realized that he was in fact not copying ancient texts at all. He was copying copies made by other monks, who no doubt had also spent their lives copying copies of the word of God.

In his enthusiasm and curiosity, he asked the abbot if it would be possible to check the original texts, which were stored deep in the vaults of the monastery. After all, he reasoned, if any mistakes had been made in the copies, they were now being spread from generation to generation.

The old abbot declined his request. He told the young monk not to worry about such things, and the young monk dutifully obeyed.

Years passed and the young monk was no longer young. Although his enthusiasm for life had somewhat diminished over the years, his hard work and years of dutiful service led to his being chosen as the new abbot when the old one died. Now, instead of filling his days copying ancient wisdom by rote, he found himself with time for contemplation and reflection. Soon his old curiosity and thirst for truth returned, and he took it upon himself to go down into the vaults at the heart of the monastery.

He stayed down there for months, poring over the ancient texts by candlelight, pausing only to pray, to sleep, and to eat the meals that were left outside the door of the vaults every morning.

One day when the young monk assigned to care for him came by to gather up the empty dishes, he heard what sounded like distant crying. Although going down into the vaults was strictly forbidden, he opened the door, lit a candle, and made his way into the sacred heart of the monastery. There he found his beloved new abbot sobbing uncontrollably.

'What's the matter, brother?' the young monk asked the abbot.

The weary abbot looked hopelessly up into the gentle eyes of the young monk. 'We've made a terrible mistake,' he said. 'The original word was "celebrate"...'

A SIMPLE WAY OF UNDERSTANDING YOUR FEELINGS

Have you ever been in a stressful situation? Seen a powerful movie? Read a sad novel or an inspiring book?

I can guarantee that you haven't, because each one of those qualities – stress, power, sadness, and inspiration – is actually *inside* you, not part of the event or object to which you're attributing it. You're the one *experiencing* the stress, power, sadness, and inspiration, and as we've been exploring throughout this book, you're even the one dreaming them in your own mind.

Here's another way of getting at it:

> Do you think your life would be better if
> your circumstances were different?

Most people say 'Of course it would.' But how then to explain the almost random distribution of happiness amongst your peer group? Do you know people who seem to have it all but it's never enough? Or people who never seem able to catch a break but always seem to find the time to stop and smell the roses? Why do some children turn up their nose at the latest toy, while others can play contentedly for hours with the box?

On the whole, when I first point this out to people, they seem to 'sort of get it.' They can certainly see that their thinking has something to do with why they experience things in particular ways, but when push comes to shove, pretty much everyone has certain exceptions to the rule – things in their life that look as though they are inherently painful, stressful, scary, or sad.

After all, wouldn't anyone get upset when they fail a test, lose the big game, or get dumped or cheated on by someone they love? And aren't some things just naturally stressful, like being diagnosed with an illness, running low on money, or having to speak in front of a group?

Well, no. Not everyone reacts to things in the same way. Some people genuinely thrive in situations that look difficult and overwhelming to others. And while it may be normal to feel insecure on the first day of a new job or sad when your football team loses, 'normal' is often a long, long way from 'natural.'

Here's our fifth secret, the secret of understanding your feelings:

> Every feeling you experience is the shadow
> of a thought, not a reflection of the world
> around you. You're living in the feeling of your
> thinking, not the feeling of your circumstances.

The more clearly you see that you're always feeling your thinking, not the world, the easier it is to simply feel your feelings without adding in a story about why you're feeling them and how long they're going to last. And the gift of that insight is that you stop needing to change the world in order to change the way you feel.

One of the most hopeful things I have realized over the past decade of studying and teaching the principles behind the inside-out understanding is that not only do my circumstances not have the power to make me feel a certain way, they don't even have the power to make me think about them. And while I don't control my thoughts, they don't control me either.

THERE'S NO SUCH THING AS A 'BAD DAY'

'We should be graceful with our low moods and grateful for our high ones.'
RICHARD CARLSON

In Beth Henley's award-winning comedy *Crimes of the Heart*, three women reunite at their old family home to deal with the troubles in their lives, ranging from their mother's suicide to the youngest daughter's attempted murder of her wealthy fiancé. In the end, they draw the conclusion that both the suicide and the attempted murder stemmed from the women in question having 'a really, really bad day.'

When all their stories have been shared and a new level of understanding has been reached, the middle daughter comes to a remarkably unremarkable solution to all their problems: 'We've just got to learn to get through these really bad days.'

At our best, we all handle life remarkably well. We know what to do and tend to do it when it needs to be done. We follow our common sense and our wisdom and naturally make the best decisions we can based on the information we have. But unfortunately, we don't always live life at our best. In fact, for many people the times spent in the comfort and care of their own wisdom and wellbeing seem far too few and far between.

Here's the thing: regardless of which gods we pray to and what we do or don't do, stuff is still going to happen that we wouldn't choose. People we love are going to get sick, our bills will come due, and things often won't turn out as planned or hoped for. As Syd Banks often said, 'Life is a contact sport – you're going to get your knocks.'

So how does knowing that we're living in the feeling of our thinking help us?

Here's a corollary to the secret of understanding your feelings:

> ### Your day doesn't create your mood; your mood creates your day.

♦ When your mood is low, the world looks bleak; when your mood is high, you feel as if you can take over the world.

♦ When your mood is high, your partner is the most wonderful person in the world; when your mood is low, they're a complete bastard.

♦ When your mood is low, you're filled with doubt; when your mood is high, you fill up with hope and possibility.

The difference is not in the world, but inside you. And a deeper understanding of how it's being created will make it easier to feel whatever you're feeling without having to cut off from unpleasant feelings or chase after pleasant ones. In other words, as we discovered in Session One, you think you have a reality problem when in reality you have a thinking problem.

Thinking problems are pretty common. Unrecognized thought can create mountains out of molehills and monsters out of thin air, obscuring whatever common sense actions we might otherwise take to make our circumstances more manageable and easier to bear. But recognizing that we can only ever suffer from our own thinking turns out to be wonderful news. Because the energy of Thought is transient, our thought-created dream of life can change for the better in any moment.

Better still, we don't even have to do the changing. As soon as we wake up to the fact that we're feeling our thinking, not our circumstances, our thoughts begin to change by themselves. It's almost as if we have a psychological immune system that, as soon as it's alerted to the fact that unhelpful thinking has taken root, weeds out old unhelpful thoughts and replaces them with fresh new ones.

But as long as we hang on to the idea that there might be exceptions to the inside-out nature of experience, the psychological immune system isn't alerted. It waits to see if this is a 'thinking problem' or a 'reality problem' before stepping in to begin the process of change. And as long as it seems to us as though we have very sound external reasons for the way that we feel, our difficulties and suffering will carry on relatively unabated.

When I first introduce people to the principles behind the human experience, they sometimes think just reading about them should work like a wizardly incantation that magically changes their life for the better. But all the principles 'do' is explain how the dream of life gets created. They don't stop you from dreaming any more than understanding the principle of gravity stops you from falling down.

So will you still slam your hand in the car door of your thinking from time to time? Absolutely. But the moment you recognize your thinking as the only possible cause of your suffering, it's surprisingly easy to stop, let new thoughts come to mind, and wake back up to the world of infinite possibility that surrounds you.

WHY NOT JUST 'THINK POSITIVE'?

> *'Our feelings are the barometer of the soul... They let us know what mental weather we can expect.'*
> SYD BANKS

Since our emotions are the shadows of our thoughts, logic suggests that the only thing that will change the way we feel is a change in the way we think. So why not just think positive all day long, carefully weeding out all the negative thoughts until your garden of positivity is lush and you can live happily ever after?

Well, first off, have you ever actually tried that?

There is a famous episode of the television series *I Love Lucy* where Lucille Ball's character gets a job working on the production line at a chocolate factory. She's supposed to wrap each chocolate as it passes by, but once one gets by her and she tries to catch up, all the other chocolates start to pile up until she and the factory are a big gooey mess. That's what usually happens when we try too hard to monitor the activity inside our head. It all goes swimmingly until one thought gets by and then everything goes to hell.

This is why I've always liked the expression 'train of thought,' because it so accurately describes the way each thought that passes through our head invites us to travel with it. One thought of a childhood friend can take us on a pleasant journey all the way back down through our youth; one thought about an argument with a loved one can carry us into paroxysms of rage or daydreams of escaping into the arms of another.

Yet our thoughts are simply the principle of Thought taking the form of internal conversations and mental movies that have no power to impact our life until we charge them up by deciding they're important and real. And if we 'empower' the wrong thoughts, making our negative fantasies seem more realistic than our current reality, it's like boarding a train to a destination we have no desire to actually reach.

That's why one of the most important things to realize about your thinking is this:

> Your thinking is a variable guide to reality,
> but your feelings are a foolproof guide to
> the quality of your current thinking.

Our guidance system lies not in analyzing our thoughts but in feeling our feelings. When we're feeling expansive (warm, loving, spacious, comfortable, easy, well, etc.), that's the shadow of healthy thinking and our thoughts can, on the whole, be trusted. When we're feeling contracted (insecure, apathetic, frustrated, numb, stressed out, uncomfortable, and so on), chances are that our thinking is unproductive and whichever train of thought we might engage with will lead us somewhere we don't really want to go.

This gives us a remarkably reliable way of navigating through to our own wisdom. We can actually use our feelings as a sort of early warning system, like a traffic signal for trains of thought:

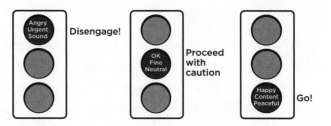

♦ If you're in a low mood, that's like a red light warning you to take a moment to stop taking your thinking so seriously. You don't have to try to change your thoughts or fix your feelings; just don't climb on the train and don't fall for the sense of importance and sudden compelling urgency many of your thoughts may seem to have.

♦ If you're feeling somewhat neutral or a bit flat, that's like a yellow light that says, 'Proceed with caution.' It's possible that some of the thoughts racing through your mind are worth paying attention to, but if you feel your mood begin to drop, jump off whatever train of thought you've been traveling on and wait until your mood rises before you re-engage with your thinking.

♦ If you're feeling relatively content, expansive, and at peace, those feelings are the shadows of higher-quality thoughts – and, while they're still made up, those thoughts can take you to some pretty wonderful places.

Of course, one of the problems with being in a low mood is that your point of view is often so distorted that you don't realize you're in a low mood!

Here are some pretty reliable indicators:

♦ You feel low or flat.

♦ Your sense of humor has gone missing.

♦ You're filled with doubts.

♦ You feel distant from the people around you.

♦ You have an all-or-nothing mentality, coupled with a sense of either urgency or *ennui*. You either feel that you must put an end to all your problems now or you feel that there's no point in doing anything about anything.

What I've seen for myself is that the feeling of urgency is one of the most reliable indicators that what I actually need to do is slow down and take a break. No matter how urgent or pressing a course of action may seem, I know that sense of urgency can only be made of thought and will come and go as thought changes. And rather than try to change my state when I'm feeling low, I do my best just to stay present, knowing that the moment my thinking changes, my feeling will change with it.

In *The Space Within*, I share the story of how as a teenager I finally learned to recognize the difference between the suicidal trains of thought that had carried along my thinking for years and any actual desire to end my life. Once I recognized the 'suicide thought' was just a thought, no more significant than any other, it naturally began to pass through each time it arose. By not 'getting on the train,' my sense of fear and suffering diminished literally overnight.

In the same way, if you don't act on your thinking when you're feeling low, you'll find that as your mood lifts, the quality of your thinking will lift with it – and when you climb aboard a quality train of thought, it can take you a long way toward living the life of your dreams.

This is sometimes easiest to recognize in the case of small children. For example, my daughter Maisy came into our bed one night, sobbing that she'd dreamed that our cat had died and we'd had to bury her. No amount of reassurance (including the presence of the actual cat) would calm her until my wife agreed to remove the dream from Maisy's head. (For those of you not familiar with this process, we've found that it is most effectively done through the ear after a bit of struggle and accompanying sound effects!)

When I checked in to see how Maisy was doing the next morning, she told me that although the dream had indeed been successfully removed, she was still able to imagine the cat dying, which made her very, very sad.

And herein lies the point:

It's not the thoughts that pass through your
head that impact your life; it's the ones you
take possession of and think about all day long.

Supercoaching Tip
Thought Recognition

During the day, if you notice yourself feeling down or a bit worried or unsettled, see if you can stay 'before the because.' That is, don't start coming up with reasons for why you feel the way you're feeling, just feel them. You'll notice them start to change at the speed of Thought they're made of!

Thought without a Thinker

Here's an example of the typical thoughts that might pass through someone's head in any given minute on the way to work in the morning:

> *I'm going to be late, I just know I'm going to be late, I*
> *shouldn't have eaten that extra piece of cake last night,*
> *I'm such a fat disgusting slob, no wonder no one will ever*
> *find me attractive, boy, he is gorgeous, I wonder what it*
> *would be like to be with someone like that, I bet it would*
> *be wonderful, I have so much love inside me – it feels really*
> *good, but no one will ever know because I'm all alone,*
> *what was the name of that song I heard on the radio last*
> *night, oh no, I'm going to be late…*

Now, in and of themselves those thoughts are not a problem.

You might experience a slight boost in your feelings when the happier thoughts float by and a slight dip in your mood when the more negative ones pass through, but if you let each thought pass without thinking about it too much, the thought stream will simply flow on quietly in the background throughout your day. But when you step in and start to actively think about thoughts, they can become a problem. For example:

> *I'm going to be late, I just know I'm going to be late, I shouldn't have eaten that extra piece of cake last night, I'm a fat disgusting slob, no wonder no one will ever find me attractive – why is this always the way? If only I had more willpower, I'm definitely going on that diet tomorrow, but what's the point, I never stick to anything, I'm such a loser … I need more cake!*

It's easy to imagine where this train of thought might take you and the associated feelings and potentially poor decisions that could follow from it. The Toltec shaman Don Miguel Ruiz describes this phenomenon as being 'hooked' by a thought – and once we agree to give our attention to a thought, it becomes more and more real to us over time and has more and more power over our life.

The trick (if you want a less stressful, more enjoyable life) is not to call in the thought police, but rather to see your thinking for what it is – the energy of Thought taking form. If you let even the most negative thought pass through your head without giving it a second thought (or a third, or fourth, or even 50th), it will have no impact on your life. But if you get hooked by it, dwell on it, make it important, and start to think about it and claim it for your own, then you'll become subject to its inevitable effects.

On the other hand, when you see through the dream of your Thought-created realities, you wake up to the deepest part of yourself – your pure unconditioned nature, sometimes talked about as your 'soul.'

Here's how Syd Banks described it in his entry in Richard Carlson and Ben Shield's anthology of spiritual wisdom, *Handbook for the Soul*:

> *The Soul is the only true source of spiritual nourishment. There are many ways to connect with and rekindle your relationship with your soul, but the most effective way is to rid yourself of the obstacles that come between you and your purity of thought.*
>
> *You can begin the process of nourishing the soul by living in the present moment, in the now. And if your mind wanders, don't take these thoughts too seriously. Just let them go, realize that they are nothing more than fleeting thoughts, and you will soon be on your way to finding the peace of mind you seek, with loving feelings for yourself and others bringing joy and contentment to your world.*

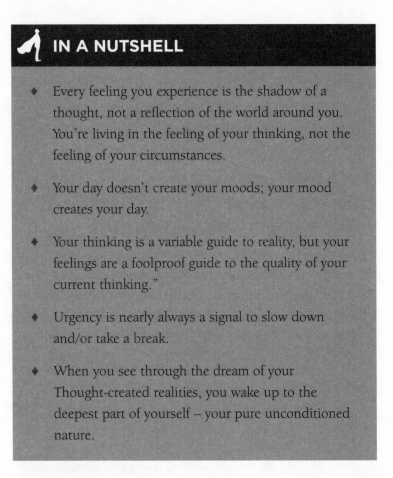

IN A NUTSHELL

♦ Every feeling you experience is the shadow of a thought, not a reflection of the world around you. You're living in the feeling of your thinking, not the feeling of your circumstances.

♦ Your day doesn't create your moods; your mood creates your day.

♦ Your thinking is a variable guide to reality, but your feelings are a foolproof guide to the quality of your current thinking."

♦ Urgency is nearly always a signal to slow down and/or take a break.

♦ When you see through the dream of your Thought-created realities, you wake up to the deepest part of yourself – your pure unconditioned nature.

If you're feeling desperate to move on to the next session, now would be a great time to take a little break. Slow down and smell the roses, or the cheese, or whatever it is you like to smell.

When you're feeling as though you could take it or leave it, it's probably time to begin the next session and our exploration of...

HOW TO GET STUFF DONE

*'There is chaos under the heavens
and the situation is excellent.'*

Chinese proverb

THE GENERAL AND THE CEO

A four-star general was taking a tour of the company that had been hired by the military to complete a major defense contract.

Despite the CEO's assurance that this particular project would be completed on time, the general felt that the CEO's team was not 100 percent committed to getting the job done. He argued that they should remain at work and do whatever it took to succeed, even if it meant working much longer hours, taking extra time away from home and family, and putting themselves under additional personal pressure and stress. He told the CEO that understanding personnel management was like eating bacon and eggs for breakfast: the chicken was 'involved'; the pig was 'committed.'

The contractor smiled and said, 'Well, that's true, general — but the pig is dead, and the chicken is still producing eggs. I want my people to stay "involved."'

The general backed down, and the project was completed on time.

SLOW DOWN TO GET MORE DONE

'Be quick, but don't hurry.'

JOHN WOODEN

Several years ago, I had child psychologist and author Alfie Kohn as a guest on my radio show. At one point, I asked him if he had any tips on how to be a more caring and effective parent when you were in a hurry. His answer, tongue only slightly in cheek, was: 'Don't be in a hurry.'

While I laughed at the time, the more I thought about it, the more I realized what excellent advice that was, not only for parenting but for pretty much any area of life. When we're in a hurry, we tend to get sloppy and things are left undone or, worse still, half done. Our best intentions often go out the window and our values shift, with 'expediency' and 'getting stuff done' leapfrogging their way up the list above such old-fashioned priorities as 'treating people with respect,' 'getting things right the first time,' and even 'enjoying the process.'

Stress is a hurrier's constant companion, as there's never enough time and always too much to do. When time gets short, tempers get shorter, and a frayed nerve often snaps in the face of a loved one. But when we take the pressure off ourselves to be exceptional – that is, be the exception to the rule that things take time and people aren't always at their best – we recognize that 'good enough' is nearly always good enough and that if we give ourselves a bit of space and time, something new will always (yes, always) come to mind.

This doesn't mean we have to go slowly – just that when we're willing to slow down, we're often able to make much quicker progress on what matters most in our life.

While you can find any number of 'outside-in' approaches to getting more done, truly effective time management evolves naturally out of an understanding of the sixth secret:

> **You have an innate real–time responsive intelligence you can rely on to let you know what to do when it's time to do it.**

'That's insane,' one CEO told me when I first introduced this idea. 'I don't know about you, but I have responsibilities. I can't just show up and "go with the flow."'

'Why not?' I responded. 'What are you concerned might happen?'

'If I didn't have a clear set of priorities and action steps, I'd never get anything done!'

'How do you know?' I asked. 'Have you ever actually tried it?'

When he admitted that he hadn't, we set it up as a little coaching experiment. Every morning, he would designate one hour to just show up and respond to what showed up, trusting his real-time responsive intelligence to guide him. After the first week, he committed to a second week; by the end of the month, he had given four hours a day to his assistant for scheduling and blocked out the rest of his calendar for 'Inspired Action.'

For myself, I have for many years used the phrase 'the kindness of the design' to describe how well we're made – how beautifully and reliably our feelings guide us back to the sense of comfort and wellbeing that lets us know when we're resting peacefully in our own true nature. I say this despite the fact that I don't really know if there is any conscious design to our perfection, any kind of designer behind the scenes, or indeed if my personal conception of 'kindness' has anything to do with it. What I do know is that it seems incredibly kind to me that we come into the world with a built-in guidance system that helps us to stay in our lane and enjoy the incredible clarity, creativity, and peace of mind that make life a joy to live instead of a struggle to endure. At times this guidance system operates like an inner GPS, giving me directions and letting me know what to do when; at other times it seems to me to operate almost like a 'homing mechanism,' telling me exactly what I need to do to calm my restless thinking, quieten my occasionally jangly nerves, and find my way back home.

What I've begun to see more and more clearly is that the intelligence of the deeper mind doesn't just guide us. It also knows how to live us. At our best, we are being lived by the higher/deeper mind. We don't need to remember everything because reminders are built into the unfolding intelligence. When we need to send an email, it will occur to us to send an email. If our thoughts are spinning out of control, it will occur to us to take a break. And if it would be helpful to us to implement a more formal time-management system, it will occur to us to do just that.

Our wisdom is already unfolding as if by design. There's nothing we need to remember or do, because it will always occur to us to do things at the genuinely perfect time to get them done.

But in the same way that the GPS in our car lets us know when there's something for us to do but stays silent the rest of the time, our innate intelligence is there when we need it but can be disconcertingly quiet when there's nothing for it to say. That in turn can lead us to doubt its existence, or at the very least its reliability. But if you reflect back through your life, you'll start to notice all sorts of examples of that real-time responsive intelligence in action.

Supercoaching Tip
Noticing the GPS

For the next few days, I invite you to notice where this innate intelligence is already at work in your own life – how often just the right thing occurs to you at just the right time for it to occur.

What would it be like if you began to rely on it to guide you? How much easier would your life be if you didn't need to be in charge of keeping yourself on track from day to day and moment to moment?

IN PRAISE OF 'AVERAGE'

Of course, sometimes we struggle to get stuff done because we're trying to do too much stuff. I remember saying goodbye to my friend and colleague Steve Chandler once when he said to me, 'Have an average day!' A bit taken aback, I asked him what he meant. After all, isn't the idea to have 'great' days, or even 'exceptional' ones?

He then told me the story of one of his mentors, a man named Lyndon Duke, who had studied something called 'the linguistics of suicide.' After receiving his doctorate, Duke had begun analyzing suicide notes to look for linguistic clues that could be used to predict and prevent suicidal behavior in teenagers. In his research, he came across the work of Dr Abraham Low, a contemporary of Jung and Adler who had developed his own somewhat controversial form of psychotherapy in the 1930s. Low worked with his patients to recognize that whatever unique skills or talents they might have, they were essentially human beings just like everyone else, dealing with the same problems in the best way they knew how. He called this the 'average person' approach to life and contrasted it with what he called 'the curse of exceptionality.'

In a world where everyone is trying to be exceptional, two things happen. The first is that nearly everyone fails, because by definition, if too many people become exceptional, the exceptional becomes commonplace. The second is that the few who do succeed feel even more isolated and estranged from their peers than before. Consequently, you have a few people feeling envied, misunderstood, and alone and tens of thousands of others feeling like failures for not being 'enough' – 'good enough,' 'special enough,' 'rich enough,' or even 'happy enough.'

This resonated deeply with my own experience. When I was in the midst of the thickest cloud of suicidal thoughts in college,

I remember wishing I could run away from my Presidential scholarship and hide, perhaps changing my name to 'Bob' and taking a job pumping gas at a service station somewhere in the Midwest. Only in my fantasy sooner or later people would start to notice that there was something special about me. They would begin driving miles out of their way to have their cars filled up by 'Bob the service guy' and exchange a few words with him, leaving the station oddly uplifted and with a renewed sense of optimism and purpose. Before long, someone would discover how exceptional I was, and I'd have to run away from their expectations all over again. I was, to my way of thinking, doomed to succeed.

Delusions of grandeur? Quite possibly. Depressed, hopeless, and miserable? Absolutely!

One of Lyndon Duke's major breakthroughs came when he was dealing with his own discontent and heard the sound of a neighbor singing while mowing his lawn. He realized then that despite all the 'exceptional' work he was doing, what was missing from his life were the simple pleasures of an average life.

The very next weekend, he went to visit his son, who was struggling to excel in his first university term. He sat him down and told him about his revised expectations for him: 'I expect you to be a straight-"C" student, young man. I want you to complete your unremarkable academic career, meet an ordinary young woman, and, if you choose to, get married and live a completely average life!'

His son thought Dad had finally flipped, but did take the pressure off himself to be quite so exceptional.

A month later he phoned his father to apologize. He'd gotten 'A's in all his exams, but it was okay because he'd only done an average amount of studying.

And this is the paradoxical promise of the 'average day' philosophy – the cumulative effect of a series of average days spent doing an average amount of what one loves and wants to do is actually quite extraordinary.

When I first introduce the notion of having an 'average day' to my clients, they often freak out at the idea of settling for average after a lifetime of successful (or unsuccessful) overachievement. To show them how much they can actually get done over a series of 'average days,' I sometimes guide them through the following exercise:

One Day at a Time

Choose an area of your life you've been trying to excel in – for example:

- writing

- sales

- being a parent

What would constitute an average day in that area? Not typical, but average, as in neither exceptionally good nor exceptionally bad? For example:

- *Writing:* Spending 45 minutes a day actually writing.

- *Sales:* Speaking to five new prospects.

- *Being a parent:* Spending at least 45 minutes before and after school focused 100 percent on being with the kids.

Project forward into the future – if you did nothing but repeat your 'average day' five days a week, how much progress would you have made in three months? A year? Five years? A lifetime? For example:

- 'Writing for 100 or so hours over a six-month period would probably be enough to complete an entire book; 200 hours a year would be enough to add some poetry and a screenplay. Writing more than 1,000 hours over a five-year period would make me prolific.'

- 'Speaking to more than 100 people a month about the difference I could make for them would definitely lead to some sales; more than 1,200 difference-making conversations a year would lead to numerous sales (and an incredible amount of skill development); more than 6,000 difference-making conversations in a five-year period would make me rich!'

- 'Spending at least 90 minutes a day with my kids each day would be more than 125 hours in three months, which would be more than enough time to really get to know them and tune in to their wants and needs; 500-plus focused hours of time spent with my children over the course of a year would create an incredible level of friendly intimacy and positive familiarity; if I made even a tiny difference in each one of nearly 3,000 hours over a five-year period, the impact on their lives and the sense of meaning in mine would be anything but average!'

Do three small things today that make a positive difference on a project you're working on or a direction you're moving in. Repeat daily for as long as you like!

THE STRANGEST DISCIPLINE

When I ask my clients what they think is really holding them back from getting things done, the most frequent answer I get is: 'A lack of discipline.'

When I ask them which disciplines specifically they feel they're lacking in, they tend to come back to me with some variations on these common themes:

♦ 'Being in a positive state of mind.'

♦ 'Taking daily action.'

♦ 'Doing the hard thing first.'

♦ 'Staying focused.'

♦ 'Feeling the fear and doing it anyway.'

While any one of the above ideas might turn out to be helpful in any given moment, I've found that the discipline that makes the biggest difference is the strangest-sounding one of them all:

> *Being disciplined enough to not do what you don't want*
> *to do, even if everyone around you (and that voice inside*
> *your head) is telling you that you should.*

Now at first glance this may seem like an 'anti-discipline' – after all, many success primers tell us that making ourselves do what we don't want to do is the very basis of successful living. But the kind of success that's built on unhappy action is like opening an empty present – you rip off the bow, tear through the beautiful wrapping, and discover there's nothing left inside.

When you're willing to consistently not do what you don't want to do, you may find yourself:

♦ Doing less but accomplishing more.

♦ Spending more time with fewer people.

♦ Burning more brightly without burning out.

This is the discipline of trusting your own innate wisdom – of consistently choosing your inner knowing over outer knowledge. It's the discipline that keeps your kids from drinking or doing drugs even though their 'friends' are telling them how cool it is, and that keeps you from jumping into business (or into bed) with the project or person who looks right but feels wrong.

In fact, in researcher Marcus Buckingham's study of people who had made a consistent positive contribution to their fields over a period of at least 20 years, the popular management consultant and bestselling author discovered that the one common element underlying their sustained personal success was this:

> They figured out what they didn't like doing and stopped doing it.

Why would anyone ever choose to do anything they didn't want to do in the first place?

Two reasons:

1. Because they think it's necessary in order to get or maintain something that they want.

2. In order to live up to an idea of how they're supposed to be in the world.

In other words, we do what we do (and don't do what we don't do) either because it seems like a good idea at the time (i.e. because we 'want' to), because we think it's a prerequisite for getting something else that we want (in other words, because we 'have' to), or because we think it will make us into the kind of person we're supposed to be (i.e. because we 'should').

I remember one journalist confronting me about this during an interview.

'It was my boyfriend's birthday last night,' she began. 'I didn't want to go out for the evening, but I knew he'd be really mad at me if I didn't. Are you saying I shouldn't have gone? He would have had a fit!'

I smiled at her earnestness. 'Perhaps,' I suggested as gently as I could, 'you could begin by not doing the things you don't want to do that no one else really cares about. Sometimes it's easier when you're the only one who knows. Besides, have you ever really regretted not doing something you didn't want to do in the first place?'

While she did acknowledge the common sense nature of my reply, there are a couple of things my clients and I have learned that make it easier not to do what you don't want to do:

1. *Need less.* So many of us have learned to motivate ourselves through our apparent needs. The idea that 'neediness' is a more powerful motivating force than inspiration is rife in our cultural mythology. In fact, many of us have spent so many years motivating ourselves through our apparent needs that being 'needy' almost feels normal. But if you want to experiment with a simpler, happier way of going for, getting, and having what you want, begin by examining how many of your 'needs' are simply things you want and have promised yourself to feel bad about if you don't get.

2. *Love more.* While I'm not a gardener, I've been told on many occasions that if you pull up weeds but don't fill your garden with flowers, the weeds will come back. In a similar way, if you develop the discipline of not doing what you don't want to do without simultaneously doing more of what you love, you may find the same unsavory choices continuing to fill your action menu.

When you're doing what you love (and loving what you do), you'll naturally tend to engage in each of the main time-management strategies currently being touted in the marketplace:

♦ You'll schedule your day (because otherwise you'd work all 24 hours).

♦ You'll say 'no' to most things (because you're already doing what you love).

♦ You'll either fall in love with or get help with the stuff you don't love (so you can spend more time doing what you love).

♦ You'll gladly sacrifice a bit of efficiency (for the joy of getting to engage fully in whatever it is that you're doing).

♦ You'll do one thing at a time (because it's so wonderful for you to take the time to do it).

Supercoaching Tip
Break Time

Whenever you're feeling that everything is spinning out of control, it's a perfect time to take a little break and slow down. Stop trying to be the exception to the rule that things take time and people aren't always at their best, and give yourself some space and time for something new to come to mind.

As the sign outside Logan Airport in Boston read for nearly seven years:

> *'Rome wasn't built in a day. If it had been,*
> *we would've used their contractors.'*

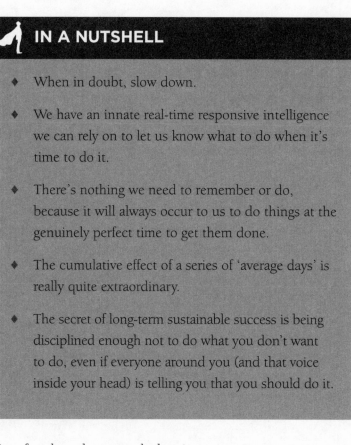

IN A NUTSHELL

+ When in doubt, slow down.

+ We have an innate real-time responsive intelligence we can rely on to let us know what to do when it's time to do it.

+ There's nothing we need to remember or do, because it will always occur to us to do things at the genuinely perfect time to get them done.

+ The cumulative effect of a series of 'average days' is really quite extraordinary.

+ The secret of long-term sustainable success is being disciplined enough not to do what you don't want to do, even if everyone around you (and that voice inside your head) is telling you that you should do it.

Have fun, learn heaps, and when it occurs to you to move on to the next session, I'll see you there!

Session Seven

THE MAGIC OF CONNECTION

'I honor the place in you where the entire universe resides. I honor the place in you of love, of truth, of peace, and of light. And when you are in that place in you and I am in that place in me, there is only one of us.'

A definition of the word *Namaste*

VAUDEVILLE

Fred: Hey, George? I say, I say, is that you, George?

George: Why, hello Fred!

Fred: I say, George, do you know that you have a banana in your ear?

George: [loudly] What was that, Fred?

Fred: I said, you have a banana in your ear, George. A great big yellow banana right there in your ear.

George: [even more loudly] What are you saying, Fred?

Fred: [yelling] Will you please take that banana out of your ear, George?!

George: [yelling back] I'm sorry, Fred, but you'll have to speak a little louder! I can't hear you – I have a banana in my ear!

LISTENING MADE FUN

Have you ever had your best 'Go ahead, I'm listening' face on while inside your head you're saying to yourself something like: *Oh my God, I can't believe he's telling me this for the 9 millionth time. Will he ever learn? What day is it today? Is it Tuesday? I wonder if there'll be something good on television tonight...?*

As you may have noticed, when we get caught up in our thoughts, we not only lose track of what another person is saying to us, we often lose the plot altogether. Yet most of us habitually go inside our head while 'listening' in order to formulate our response to what's being said. This is roughly akin to looking for your keys inside the house instead of out in the street because the lighting's better indoors. But if the keys are outside, you won't find them on the inside, no matter how well illuminated things may appear.

While this may seem harmless enough now and then, when it becomes habitual, it can be the beginning of the end for a great many relationships, both business and personal. For example, I was once having a discussion with a potential client who was struggling with her husband's lack of emotional availability. While she didn't want to get a divorce, neither did she want to, as she put it, 'live with an emotional corpse' for the rest of her life.

She was explaining all the ways in which her husband's lack of emotional intelligence manifested itself when I stopped her.

'You sound like a trial lawyer making her closing argument,' I said.

'Actually, that was just my opening argument!' she replied.

I laughed, but she didn't, so I asked her if she'd ever come across the once popular relationship book for women called *The Rules*.

'I think so,' she said. 'Wasn't that the one that told you how many days to wait before phoning a guy back, when not to say "I love you" and things like that?'

'That's the one,' I said. 'There's also one for guys called *The Game*, which claims to lay out the way for men to get around the rules. The problem with both of those books, and in fact any system that claims to teach you how to "win the game of love," is this:

When it comes to relationships, if you're playing to win, you've already lost.

The same thing is true here. It doesn't matter how good a "case" you can build against your husband – if you keep putting your partner on trial, you may win the arguments, but you'll ultimately lose the relationship.'

Something about the directness of that seemed to strike her, and her voice softened as she asked me, 'So how am I supposed to stop doing it?'

'That's the beauty of it,' I pointed out. 'You don't have to. All you have to do is recognize when it's happening and not take it so seriously. It will pass, and before you know it you'll be right back to the heart of any relationship – the deep feeling of love, connection, and wellbeing that makes being in a long-term committed relationship so wonderful.'

She thought about that for a few moments and then asked, with a smile in her voice, 'But what if I have a really strong case?'

This time we both laughed, and I pointed out that in relation to our thinking, we have a choice:

> We can entertain our thoughts or we
> can let our thoughts entertain us.

Enjoy Your Thoughts

Here are a couple of things you can do to begin to enjoy your habitual thoughts instead of being distracted by them:

- Imagine you're actually about to enter a courtroom to 'make the case' against the person you're having trouble with. How have they wronged you? In what ways have you been maligned and misunderstood? Play with turning up the heat on your case until it begins to sound like a country music song. You'll know you've cranked it up enough when it begins to make you smile instead of scowl.

- Notice what happens to your experience when you recognize that it's not the other person but your thoughts about the other person that are driving you nuts.

THE SECRET OF CONNECTION

Connection is the secret of all great relationships, but connecting is a deceptive skill because there's no actual skill involved at all. When it comes to our relationships, the secret we'll be exploring in this session is this:

Connection is what happens when human
beings spend time together without
their thinking getting in the way.

We are born into the oneness of life and then move into a
separate reality as our thought system begins to take form. But
just underneath the thoughts that separate and individuate
us is the singular energy that we're made of. And while most
of us have experienced moments of absolute oneness with a
baby, a lover, or some aspect of nature, an even more common
experience is the sense of connection when we're with other
people without too much on our mind. It's only when our
thinking is running amok that we start to feel truly separate or
even distant from one another. This is because our relationships
with other people unfold almost entirely in our head.

When we think about a person, we aren't actually thinking
about the 'real' them – we're thinking about a representation
of them we've formed in our mind, like an icon on a computer.
Our thoughts are literally making them up in our mind.

At some point, we decide what people are 'really like,' and from
that moment on we maintain them in our minds as a fixed
persona. We then look and listen for the person we expect to
see and hear, filtering out anything that doesn't fit with the
character we've created for that individual.

'So you're saying that I'm creating my husband as a miserable,
moody, self-righteous pain in the ass?' one woman asked me.

'Absolutely,' I replied. 'How's that working out for you?'

When it comes to enjoying great relationships, the thing to remember is this:

There are four of you in every couple, and two of you are really in the way.

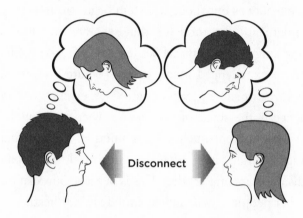

This isn't just true in one-on-one relationships. I experience this all the time with audiences when I teach – I somehow manage to fall in love with a room full of strangers simply because I'm being with them instead of being with my thinking. When I do get caught up in my head – either because I'm too nervous or too confident or too distracted – I can still bluster my way through a talk, but the intimacy, magic, and connection are lost. Speaking becomes a job, and while the audience may still enjoy what I have to say, their experience of what I have to offer will be a considerably more limited one.

It is this quality of connection that makes romantic love so intoxicating and allows new parents to stare into their baby's eyes for hours on end. To simply be with someone or something in a state of full presence is one of the most magical gifts we're given in our life, and one that for most of us is under-received because we don't recognize our part in its presence or absence.

To get a taste of this for yourself, try this exercise, based on the work of public speaker and former stand-up comedian Lee Glickstein:

Being With

- Take a few moments to center yourself. You may want to take three slow and gentle breaths with your eyes closed and simply be with yourself.

- Now open your eyes and choose any object in the space you're currently in. Take a minute or so to 'be with' that object – that is, allow yourself to become fully present to it, as if it were the most important thing in the world.

- When you get the hang of this, you'll feel a sense of being completely present with it – as though you and the object are connected in some way.

- When you're familiar with what it feels like to 'be with' an object, try it with a friend (or in a pinch, a beloved pet!) Just take a couple of moments to get out of your head, and then simply 'be with' each other, without words and without effort. Don't worry if it feels awkward or uncomfortable at first – you'll get past that, and the sweet feeling of connection you'll get to will be completely worth it!

- Finally, allow yourself to experiment with what it's like to 'be with' the rest of the people who are in your world. There's no formal exercise here – as you get used to being fully present with others, it will naturally begin to infuse your relationships and enhance your presence in the world.

Of course, you don't have to 'be with' everyone – but isn't it nice to know that you could?

LEARN TO LISTEN, LISTEN TO LEARN

'...and words are dangerous, because you might listen to them. And that would be a mistake.'
RAM DASS

There's an old joke about a therapist who operated on the theory that all problems could be traced to dreaming about fish. A patient came to him complaining about his lackluster sexual relations with his wife. Here's a transcript of their first session together:

Patient: My wife and I just aren't getting along, doctor, you know, in bed. Between my work schedule and her dealing with the kids, it just feels as if the magic's gone.

Therapist: Hmm ... tell me, do you ever dream?

P: Uh – sure I dream.

T: Tell me your most recent dream.

P: Well, I don't remember much. I was walking down a city street, and there were lots of tall buildings and cars but no people.

T: Had it been raining?

P: Not sure – I guess it might have been.

T: So there were puddles?

P: I suppose there could have been puddles.

T: And, I'm just guessing here, might there have been fish in those puddles?

P: Wow – I suppose there might have been…

T: [triumphant] Aha! Just as I suspected – fish in the dreams!

While most of our own biases aren't so obvious and don't seem so silly (at least to us), the point is that if you're listening for something specific, you'll tend to hear it. Listen for hesitation in the voice of your partner and – boom! – you've 'caught' your mate lying to you. Listen for warning signs of trouble in your relationship and before you know it, they'll be everywhere.

The problem doesn't so much have to do with what you're listening for, but what you'll miss by listening for it. Whether it's the affection in your partner's voice, the look of love in their eyes, or the heaviness in your child's heart when they're telling you about what happened at school today, if you're listening too hard for something else, you're liable to miss what's actually there. But as soon as you expand your listening palette, you'll be able to hear more and more.

There's an exercise I do near the beginning of every Supercoach Academy training where I ask participants to deliberately listen to one another in three distinct ways:

1. Listening to affirm

One of my favorite movie scenes is the moment in *Pretty Woman* where the salesperson in the posh Beverly Hills clothing store realizes that Julia Roberts is not a poor street urchin wasting his time but actually the girlfriend of mega-millionaire Richard Gere's Edward Lewis. He suddenly becomes the most attentive man in the world, nodding his head in continual agreement with everything Gere and Roberts say like a bobblehead doll. After a few minutes, he checks back in with 'Mr. Lewis' to see how he's doing. When Gere suggests the need for more sucking up, the salesperson begins complimenting him on his manliness, to which Gere responds with disbelief 'Not me – her!'

When we listen to affirm, we do it with the best of intentions. We want to make sure the person knows we're listening and that we approve of them (or at least of their right to be who they are). But the actual effect, more often than not, is to miss what's really going on with them in an effort to make them feel that we care. And as a result, they feel disconnected from us, even if they're flattered by the level of our attentiveness.

2. Listening to negate

A less socially acceptable but equally common listening habit many of us have developed over the years is listening in a way that subtly (and not so subtly) lets the person know that while we may have to listen to them, we don't have to like it.

I remember when I first moved to Hollywood, I was at a dinner with a television director and his actress wife. The wife studiously ignored me throughout the meal, talking over me and aiming her conversation at everyone else at the table. It wasn't until we were left alone together at one point that she finally made eye contact, looking me up and down as if I were a horse at auction.

When she finally spoke, it was to say, 'Are you funny?'

'What?'

'Are you funny?'

Not sure how to react, I said, 'I'm pretty funny.'

She nodded, more to herself than to me. 'That's all right then. You're good looking enough to be funny, but if you weren't funny, you're not good looking enough to be here.'

When we listen to negate, we're not just negating what the person is saying, we're often negating their right to say anything at all. The result, once again, is a sense of disconnection, this time deliberately cultivated.

3. Easy listening

'Purpose tremor' is a phrase that describes the slight shake most people notice in their hands when they first try to thread a needle or remove the shinbone in a game of Operation. Simply put, our muscles work better when we're not trying so hard to make them work better.

What's sometimes less obvious is that the same thing is true with our listening:

> It's easy to hear what's really going
> on with other people when we're not
> trying so hard to listen to them.

When I introduce this third kind of listening, I often do it by way of analogy:

♦ Listen like a video camera, without any preference for what's being recorded.

♦ Listen like a rock with ears.

♦ Listen the way you might listen to pleasant background music.

♦ Listen with nothing on your mind, as though the sound waves are simply passing through you like radio waves through the air.

At first, both the person speaking and the person listening tend to find 'just listening' a bit uncomfortable. We're so conditioned to listen to affirm or used to listening to negate that listening with nothing on our mind feels as though we're not listening at all. But after a few minutes, the ever-present underlying connection between any two human beings shows itself. The speaker often winds up feeling truly seen and heard for the first time in ages, and the listener often feels that they've known the other person for years and the conversation was like getting reacquainted with an old friend.

When you listen to another person with nothing on your mind, things will also jump out at you that turn out to be the keys to unlocking whatever is going on for that person.

And when you learn to listen to yourself in the same way, it becomes easier and easier to separate your own mental chatter from the still, small voice of wisdom within.

Try this for yourself…

Supercoaching Tip
Just Listen

1. Choose a few non-crucial conversations to experiment with this week and notice what you can about your own habitual listening filters. Are you listening to affirm or negate? For problems or opportunities? For holes in other people's arguments or openings for resolution? What they're saying with their words or what they're communicating with their feelings?

2. Just for this week, try listening to other people with nothing on your mind. Let your thoughts come and go as they will. Notice how much more you hear, both spoken and unspoken, and whether or not this actually does make the other person feel 'heard.' There's no effort necessary – just allow the words to come in and pass right through you, with nothing on your mind and no agenda as to what you want or don't want to hear.

3. As a bonus, try just listening to yourself this week. Notice if your sense of self-intimacy and connection with the deeper mind increases.

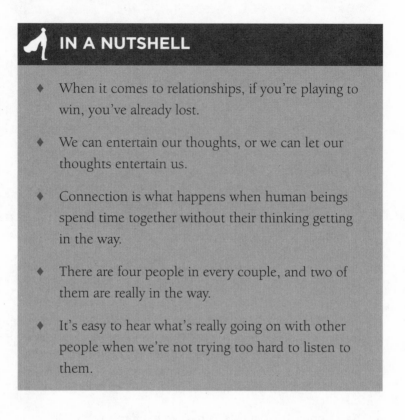

IN A NUTSHELL

◆ When it comes to relationships, if you're playing to win, you've already lost.

◆ We can entertain our thoughts, or we can let our thoughts entertain us.

◆ Connection is what happens when human beings spend time together without their thinking getting in the way.

◆ There are four people in every couple, and two of them are really in the way.

◆ It's easy to hear what's really going on with other people when we're not trying too hard to listen to them.

When you're ready, I'll be waiting for you in the very next session...

Session Eight

HOW TO ASK FOR ANYTHING FROM ANYONE

'If I had a prayer, it would be this:
"God, spare me from the desire for love,
approval, or appreciation. Amen."'
Byron Katie

THE COOKIE THIEF

A young woman was early to catch her flight home for the holidays, so she decided to get herself a snack. The smell of fresh-baked cookies caught her attention and she bought a bag full of them to help pass the time while she waited.

Although the airport was overflowing with people, a kindly looking gentleman made space for her next to him, and she gratefully sat down. After a few moments, she reached her hand down into the bag and pulled out the first of her afternoon treats. To her surprise, the 'gentleman' reached into the bag just moments later and took one of the cookies for himself.

Shocked by this rude behavior, she decided to be the bigger person and not say a word. Looking around to see if anyone had noticed, she took a second cookie out of the bag, determined to savor it. But before she had even finished the first bite, the man once again reached into the bag and took another cookie for himself.

Although she did little to disguise her displeasure, she was still shocked into silence by the boldness of his action.

This cookie thievery went on for the next few minutes like a game of tennis, with first her hand and then the stranger's dipping into the bag one after the other until there was only one cookie left.

Surely he wouldn't take the last cookie, she thought. He wouldn't dare. Would he?

But no sooner had she thought the thought than the man's hand reached into the very bottom of the bag and came out with the very last delectable cookie.

Then, to her amazement, the man smiled at her as he broke the cookie in half and handed her the larger of the two halves before leaving his seat to dispose of the cookie bag and no doubt find some other unsuspecting young woman to take advantage of.

Just then her flight was called. As she stood up to get in line to board the plane, still shaking with anger at the actions of the stranger, she noticed to her dismay a full bag of cookies, still sitting on the ground by her feet where she'd left them.

THE 'NEED' FOR APPROVAL

Steve Hardison is a somewhat legendary figure in the coaching world, not only for his incredible impact as a coach but also for the jaw-dropping fees he charges and his ability to ask pretty much anyone for pretty much anything.

One of my favorite stories about him dates back to his time as a missionary for the Mormon Church. One day he had gone up to a house and begun speaking about the Church's teachings to the man who'd answered the door when the man punched him in the face. Steve's nose began to bleed, but without missing a beat, he asked the man for a towel to help staunch the bleeding so they could continue their conversation.

What is it that allows one person to ask and ask and ask for what they want, while others stop themselves before even popping the very first question?

This is the simple secret at the heart of this session:

> You can ask anyone for anything if you
> don't buy into your thinking about what
> it would mean if they said 'no.'

Your ability to not take the word 'no' personally, no matter how dramatically that 'no' may be delivered, is the key to success – not (by definition) because people will always say 'yes,' but because it won't be unduly discouraging to you if they don't. The more comfortable you get with your thinking around hearing the word 'no,' the less likely you are to get caught up in a sort of 'post-traumatic stress disorder' of the mind, walking on eggshells and becoming more and more afraid to ask for what you want.

When you no longer fear your thinking around someone saying 'no,' you're free to consider why they didn't say 'yes.'

In my experience, there are really only three reasons why someone would say 'no' to a clear request:

1. Fear or insecurity that you will talk them into thinking about something they don't want to think about or doing something they don't want to do.

2. A lack of information or understanding about how what you're asking will be of benefit to them, either directly or indirectly.

3. A genuine knowing on their part that they don't want to be, do, or have what you're requesting.

All of these reasons are completely impersonal and nothing to do with you. If their 'no' is coming from fear, that's about their thinking and level of consciousness, not you or your external request. If it's coming from a lack of information or understanding, it's still impersonal – it's up to you whether or not to continue until they have enough information/ understanding to make an informed decision. If they're saying 'no' because they really don't want to, that's equally nothing to do with you – it's simply a statement from them to them about their willingness to trust their own intuition, awareness, and inner knowing.

Personally, I love a clear 'no,' even if I can still be somewhat taken aback if I'm not expecting it. It takes me off the hook for trying to convince them and it gets me out of 'sales' mode and back into simply asking. And, as self-help pioneer Jack Canfield says, 'Some will, some won't – so what?'

So, given how impersonal and even understandable it is that sometimes people don't do what we ask them to, why do we have so much thinking about the word 'no'?

Because when we make our requests, we tend to put our self-image, self-esteem, and even physical survival on the line along with whatever it is we're requesting. Instead of simply asking for the sale, the job, or the hand in marriage, our self-conscious subtext gets rolled into the question and what we're actually asking goes a little something like this:

> *Would you please do as I'm requesting and approve of me, affirm me as a human being, ensure I have whatever I need to survive, and let me know I'm worthy of your acceptance?*

That's a tall order for anyone, let alone someone you've never even met before.

In fact, one of the simplest ways to get past your fear of asking for what you want is to notice whether your attention is on yourself or the person you're asking. If it's on you – your self-image, self-worth, or what it might mean to you for them to say 'yes' or 'no' to your request – that self-directed, self-conscious thinking will inevitably manifest as fear or discomfort. But the moment you turn the full light of your attention onto the other person and how what you're asking will benefit and serve them, the discomfort disappears and you'll find it surprisingly easy to ask for what you want.

In order to see how self-consciousness serves as an obstacle to asking, consider going up to 100 people and either asking for something you want or selling them a product or your own services. Now, 50 of these people already know you very well – they're members of your family or friends and colleagues. The other 50 are complete strangers and don't know anything about you.

Which group would you find it easier to approach?

In my experience, people are fairly split in their answers to this question, but fewer than five in 100 would find approaching both groups to ask for what they wanted or sell their product or services an effortless, fun endeavor.

The reason is once again in our own thought-created reality. In our mind, those people will think ill of us for asking, and while we may never even know if that's true, we somehow don't want to risk it, as if another person thinking unpleasant thoughts about us can magically cause unpleasant feelings to appear in our body. But, as we discussed in our previous sessions, we can only ever feel our *own* thinking. The only mechanisms in our biology that allow us to pick up on someone else's feeling state are the mirror neurons in our frontal cortex, and when we're in a place of mental clarity, we experience that connection as compassion and empathy, not suffering and misery.

Now, imagine how much easier it would be to ask for what you wanted if your sense of wellbeing were stable enough for you not to buy into any insecure thoughts about what other people might think or do. If you knew you would be safe, happy, and well no matter what, would you care if they said 'yes' or 'no' to your request?

What we think of as a desire for approval is really a desire for safety and wellbeing, which can never be found if we continue to look in the wrong place – outside our innermost selves.

As we discussed in Session Two, happiness, wellbeing, and wisdom come from within. They aren't the fruit of something you do; they're the essence of who you are. And there's nothing you can ask for and be given from the outside that will fill the hole you've been digging for yourself on the inside.

WHO DO YOU THINK THEY ARE?

> '*In America everybody is of the opinion that he has no social superiors, since all men are equal, but he does not admit that he has no social inferiors.*'
> Bertrand Russell

I was checking into a hotel once and found myself stuck behind someone who was trying to get an upgrade by intimidating the woman behind the desk.

'You'd better be careful, lady,' the irritated asker said, 'or I'll tell you who I am!'

While I have no idea who he was, the point is that people who are caught up in their insecure thinking about asking will often resort to status, real or imagined, as a way of compensating for their own discomfort.

Supercoaching Tip
How to Ask

The best book I've ever read on the power of asking to get what you want is Jack Canfield and Mark Victor Hansen's *The Aladdin Factor*. In it, they offer the following eight suggestions for how to ask:

1. Ask as if you expect to get it.

2. Ask someone who can give it to you.

3. Be clear and specific in your requests.

4. Ask with humor and creativity.

5. Ask from the heart.

6. Be prepared to give something in order to get something.

7. Ask repeatedly.

8. Be gracious in accepting a 'no.'

One of my clients was trying to understand why she felt nervous with certain people but completely confident with others. After exploring and discarding numerous theories, we soon found that the pattern was as follows:

♦ If she felt someone was 'better' than her in some way, she felt nervous.

♦ If she felt someone was 'a bit beneath' her in some way, she felt confident.

In an impromptu and extraordinarily unscientific poll I then conducted among my friends, these were the top 10 reasons (in no particular order) for feeling superior or inferior to a fellow human being:

1. Being larger or smaller in height or weight.

2. Being physically stronger or weaker.

3. Having a degree or qualification from a better or lesser school or college.

4. Being older or younger.

5. Being more or less experienced.

6. Being more or less of an 'expert.'

7. Being more or less beautiful/handsome.

8. Achieving a higher or lower level of 'success.'

9. Earning more or less money.

10. Doing more or fewer 'good' works in the world.

So, how do you not psych yourself out in relation to someone you think is in some way better than you?

One piece of advice I've heard given to both salespeople and public speakers is that if you feel frightened when you're about to speak to an individual or a group, imagine them in their underwear or sitting on the toilet. (This does make people seem less imposing, but I've always found it kind of gross!)

An early mentor, the author Stuart Wilde, taught me a similar trick – to imagine myself 30 feet tall, towering over the 'puny people' in the audience – while Dr Richard Bandler teaches his students to imagine themselves inside the body of a sleek black puma, looking out at the world through bright yellow eyes and saying to themselves, 'Your ass is mine!'

The problem with all these 'humanizing' games is that while they do often result in reduced nerves, they tend to also result in dehumanizing the people we play them with. In fact, it's not at all uncommon to see a speaker with supreme self-confidence come off as simply arrogant. They might feel great, but their audience won't care – they won't feel connected, or in some cases even acknowledged. My feeling is that if you're going to imagine others in their underwear, do it because you find them attractive!

Although psychologist Alfred Adler once quipped, 'To be human means to feel inferior,' making a shift from feeling inferior to superior is simply trading one way of denying our shared humanity for a slightly more pleasant one.

A third option, and the one I proposed to my client, is to fall in love with your 'unique ordinariness' – a recognition of both the uniqueness of your particular separate reality and the ordinariness of having one.

If you're wondering what you have in common with the most horrible people you can imagine, the list is legion:

♦ We're all alive, aware, and we think.

♦ We're all doing the best we can, given the thinking we have that seems real to us.

♦ We're all going to die. As George Bernard Shaw said, 'Be patient with the poor people who … think they will live forever, which makes death a division instead of a bond.'

When you recognize everyone around you as being both unique and 'just like you' – no better and no worse – you open up the gateway to more love, deeper connection, and longer-lasting relationships. You may not feel as 'confident' as you would if you thought yourself to be superior, but you'll get to feel something even better – an ongoing sense of ease and wellbeing, regardless of whom you happen to be with and what you want to ask for.

OVER THE EDGE OF THE WORLD

As I mentioned earlier, one of my early mentors was Stuart Wilde. Stuart delighted in taking people to the edge of their thought-created world and, on occasion, pushing them over that edge into a larger world of fresh experiences and new possibilities.

In fact, one of the reasons you're reading this now is because Stuart pushed me. Before I'd ever run a training on my own, he asked me to go out in front of a group of people to lead a 'trust fall' as part of his 'Warrior's Wisdom' course.

For those of you who haven't done one before, a trust fall is where a group of people who don't know each other very well have to catch one another as they fall backward blindfolded off a table, a ladder, or in our case an eight-foot-high tree stump. If the group learns to work together quickly, no one gets hurt and everybody learns about the power of trust. If the group doesn't learn to work together quickly, people do get hurt and everybody learns something else.

Totally terrified by my insecure thoughts about being placed in the role of both 'teacher' and 'coach' for the first time, I asked Stuart what I was supposed to do. He said, 'It's a trust fall – tell 'em to trust and then fall!'

To make a long story short, I trusted, they fell, and 30 years later I'm still working with individuals and standing up in front of groups, a testament to the catalyzing power of being willing to follow a trusted guide out over the edge of your world (something we'll talk about further in Session Ten).

In my years of coaching and teaching since that day, I've invited thousands of clients and students to follow me out to the edge of their thought-created world and invited them to step out over that edge into uncharted waters filled with at least one mermaid for every dragon and at least one new rise for every fall. These invitations have ranged from the gentle to the extreme, but in every case have been based on my knowing that the only real obstacle to moving forward is a thought about what might happen if you do...

Supercoaching Tip
Unreasonable Requests

If you want a personal invitation to step out over the edge of your own world, here you go: for the next 30 days, make at least one 'unreasonable' request per day.

A request counts as 'unreasonable' if you can't think of any reason for the person to say 'yes.' As you go through this experiment, you may be surprised by how reasonable many of your seemingly unreasonable requests turn out to be.

Here are some of the many ways to get over yourself and go over the edge of your world:

◆ If you're someone who is habitually argumentative, seek out someone you fundamentally disagree with and have a conversation in which you completely agree with everything they say. If you're generally more of a 'go along to get along' type, find someone you like and get into an argument with them.

◆ Go into work tomorrow dressed completely differently from the way you normally dress. (Stuart used to recommend a chicken costume.) If anyone comments, just smile and go about your business.

◆ Make a list of 'forbidden' words – ones you would never even think of using in polite company. Choose a different word for each of the next seven days and work it into your conversations as often as you can.

♦ Go to a place of business and deliberately ask for a product or service you know they don't provide. Order a pizza in a Chinese restaurant. Walk into a clothing store and ask them to repair your vacuum cleaner. No matter how they react, stick with your request until you're ready to leave.

♦ Choose a store you've never been to before. Pick an item off the shelf, go to the checkout, and offer 10 percent of the asking price in cash – $1 for a $10 book, $50 for a $500 television set, and so on.

If you feel sick at the very thought of doing any or all of these things, wonderful – that means you've found the edge of your imaginary thought-created dream world. And if you realize that all uncomfortable feelings are telling you is that you've got some pretty uncomfortable thinking, you can let that thinking go as best you can and see what else comes to mind.

IN A NUTSHELL

◆ You can ask anyone for anything if you don't buy into your thinking about what it would mean if they said 'no.'

◆ A 'no' is never about you, even if the other person thinks it is.

◆ When you recognize the people around you as being both unique and 'just like you' – no better and no worse – you open up the gateway to more love, deeper connection, and longer-lasting relationships.

◆ When you look within for your sense of security and wellbeing, you never have to fear rejection.

The next time you're deciding on a course of action that involves at least one other person, try asking yourself the following question first:

*If I already had all the love in the world,
how would I do this differently?*

Have fun, learn heaps, and I'll meet you in the next session when you're ready…

Session Nine

THE SECRET TO A LIFETIME OF FINANCIAL SECURITY

'[Security] does not exist in nature, nor do the
children of men as a whole experience it...
Avoiding danger is no safer in the long run
than outright exposure... Life is either
a daring adventure or nothing.'

Helen Keller

THE RICH MAN AND THE BEGGAR

Many years ago, a man was sitting in quiet contemplation by a riverbank when he was disturbed by a beggar from the local village.

'Where is the stone?' the beggar demanded. 'I must have the precious stone!'

The man smiled up at him. 'What stone do you seek?'

'I had a dream,' the beggar answered, barely able to slow his words enough to speak, 'and in that dream a voice told me that if I went to the riverbank, I would find a man who would give me a precious stone that would end my poverty forever!'

The man looked thoughtful, then reached into his bag and pulled out a large diamond.

'I wonder if this is the stone?' he said kindly. 'I found it on the path. If you'd like it, you may certainly have it.'

The beggar couldn't believe his luck, and he snatched the stone and ran back to the village before the man could change his mind.

One year later, the beggar, now dressed in the clothes of a wealthy man, came back to the riverbank in search of his anonymous benefactor.

'You have returned, my friend!' said the man, who was again sitting in his favorite spot enjoying the peaceful flow of the water before him. 'What has happened?'

The beggar humbled himself before the man. 'Many wonderful things have happened to me because of the diamond you gave me so graciously. I have become wealthy, found a wife, and bought a home. I am now able to give employment to others and to do what I want, when I want, with whomever I want.'

'So why have you returned?' asked the man.

'Please,' the beggar said. 'Teach me whatever it is inside you that allowed you to give me that stone so freely.'

THE $600 MILLION MAN

When I first began working with high-income/high-net-worth clients, I was surprised that money came up so frequently as an issue. Men and women with six-figure incomes and millions in the bank were dealing with the same kind of fears and concerns around their finances as the people I knew with no money in the bank and no income to speak of. I would often hear phrases like:

◆ 'I don't want to, but I need the money.'

◆ 'With the economy the way it is, I don't know how I'm ever going to be able to retire.'

◆ 'I have to worry – otherwise I might lose it all!'

Apparently, having a high income or a huge bank balance had little or no impact on feeling secure about money. I actually found this quite disconcerting. I had somehow convinced myself that there was a magic number and that once my bank balance hit it, I would never have to worry about money again.

What completely divested me of that illusion was when one client whose net worth was nearly $600 million told me that he woke up every morning wondering if today was going to be the day he lost it all. It finally got through to me that if $600 million wasn't enough to guarantee financial security, $600 billion wouldn't be enough either (and neither would $600,000 or $100,000 or whatever other number had seemed to my brain at the time to be more money than I could possibly spend in a lifetime.) I remember making a little note of the first part of this session's secret to keep by my desk. It read:

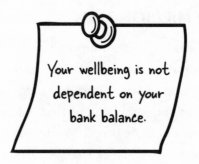

Your wellbeing is not dependent on your bank balance.

This phenomenon quite clearly worked in both directions. At the same time that I was working with my insecure millionaires, I had other clients who had far less money in the bank but didn't seem to worry about it at all.

As always, the differences between financial security and financial insecurity were being created from the inside out.

To understand a bit more about why financial security has nothing to do with your bank balance, imagine this scenario:

You live in a cold climate. Your partner asks you to put some more wood on the fire, but when you look at the woodpile, it's almost empty. What do you do next?

If you're like most people, you either go out back and chop up some more or drive down to the nearest shop and buy some. In fact, you get plenty of extra so that the next time you want to build a fire you don't have to go back out unless you want to.

Now, imagine this second scenario:

You live wherever it is that you live. Your partner asks you
if there's enough money to go on vacation this year, but
when you look at the bank account, it's almost empty.
What do you do next?

If you're like most people, you panic. You either make up excuses as to why you can't take a vacation or lay down the law about why vacations are overrated and a waste of money anyway. Secretly, you feel like a bit of a failure and resent the heck out of your partner for wanting to go in the first place (even though you'd love to get away as well). Perhaps you vow to yourself to work harder, or find a better-paying job or less demanding partner.

What's the difference between the two scenarios?

In the first, you recognize that wood is just a commodity – something you need from time to time for a specific purpose and it's easy enough to get more of with a little bit of effort.

In the second, you're acting as if money is in some way magical – something you always need more of and that would make your problems magically disappear if only you could somehow get enough of it.

But what if money were just a commodity too – something you used from time to time for a specific purpose and could easily get more of with a little bit of effort? If money were just a commodity, you wouldn't panic when you were running low, you'd simply go out and get more of it whenever there was something you wanted to buy. You might even get plenty of extra so the next time you wanted to buy something or go somewhere you didn't have to go back out unless you wanted to.

WHAT IT FEELS LIKE TO BE A MILLIONAIRE

As I worked on this session, I was reflecting on how to demonstrate the difference between creating money for its own sake and chasing after it in the hopes that it will make us feel a certain way when we catch it. Here's an exercise I used to do on my 'Financially Fearless' programs called 'The Millionaire Exercise.' If you'd like to know what if feels like to be a millionaire, do the following:

The Millionaire Exercise

Take stock of how you feel in your body right now:

- What parts of your body feel particularly relaxed or particularly tight or tense?

- What words would you use to describe your emotional state?

- Are you feeling hopeful or pessimistic? Secure or insecure?

However you are feeling in this moment is *exactly* what it feels like to be a millionaire.

The reason this is true is that we don't feel our bank balance – we feel the principle of Thought taking form, i.e. our thinking, moment by moment. And while having more than a million dollars in your bank account might lead to some new thoughts in your head, it's unlikely to make any of the old ones go away.

Yet people ascribe all sorts of magical properties to money. According to our cultural mythology, money makes you feel happy and secure, while a lack of money is the cause of feelings of frustration, anger, insecurity, and fear.

Ironically, realizing that our feelings of security will come and go regardless of our bank balance tends to make the game of creating money easier than ever to play. When we know our wellbeing is not on the line, we play full out and fearless. We spend less time in our head worrying, which leaves us with more bandwidth to both notice inspired possibilities and spot opportunities to make a difference in the lives of others in the world.

So, while you may or may not ever become a millionaire, knowing that your capacity for joy and sorrow, security and insecurity, and the innate wellbeing that lies just beneath the surface of your thinking will be unaffected by your income makes more space to follow the breadcrumbs that lead to more money coming in.

The fact is, money and wood (and metal and pork bellies) are just commodities. The difference between them is that you buy commodities with money and you 'buy' money by making a difference.

Which gives us the second part of the secret:

> Master the art of difference-making
> and you secure your financial future.

Here's a simple corollary:

> Anywhere there's a positive difference to
> be made, there's money to be made. If you
> can't (or won't) make much of a difference,
> you're unlikely to make very much money.

WHAT IS MONEY?

I've always suspected that the first official 'financial' transaction between nations involved the trade of several chickens for a goat, and that both nations (or what we would today consider to be tribes) had members who violently protested that 'our chickens are worth way more than their goats' and vice versa.

Far-fetched though that may seem, compare it to this brief and highly abridged history of currency in the modern world:

In some ancient Oceanic cultures, conch shells were used to facilitate the exchange of goods and services, as people 'shelled out' for food and lodging. Later, workers in the salt mines of Mesopotamia were paid in salt, or salarium, creating the first 'salaried' workers and no doubt the first grumblings of comparative salt envy.

As trade grew more complex, and it became completely impractical to carry shells, salt, or even chickens in your purse for barter, precious metals began to be the universal currency, leading to the establishment in the 19th century of the gold standard system that enabled easier international trade.

In the last 70 years, what we call 'money' has changed forms again, and the coins and paper we carry around are no longer backed by gold but rather by faith – our faith in the government's ability to continue to back our currency at a comparable level to other governments' ability to back theirs.

So, if what we use as money has progressed over time from chickens to shells to salt to gold to faith, what exactly is this money stuff that seems to have everyone all worked up?

Well, one answer is 'Whatever we make it up to be.' While this is essentially true (see the recent proliferation of cryptocurrencies as a startlingly modern example), it might be useful to create a shared definition, at least for the purposes of our conversation:

Money is a practical tool created to facilitate the exchange of goods and services.

When viewed in this way, much of what we believe and/or worry about money becomes nonsensical.

One of my favorite money/thought experiments involves substituting the word 'hammer' (another practical tool) for the word 'money' into many of the most limiting beliefs and ideas that are present in our culture.

Here are a few of my favorites...

♦ The love of hammers is the root of all evil.

♦ It takes hammers to make hammers.

♦ Hammers don't grow on trees.

♦ Hammers are a corrupting influence in our society.

♦ He is more important than me because he has more hammers than I do; she is less important than me because she has less hammers than I do.

So, if money is just a tool, where do we place it in our hierarchy of values? How important *should* money be in our lives?

How do we evaluate the value of a tool?

The answer is surprisingly simple: by its suitability for the job we are using it to do. How valuable is a hammer? If we are looking to pound nails into wood to construct the frame for a house (or stakes into the ground to hold up a tent), incredibly valuable. If we are looking to turn a screw, replace a lightbulb, or get a table at our favorite restaurant, not very valuable at all.

How valuable is a paintbrush? If we want to change the color of a room or forge a copy of our favorite Picasso, indispensable. If we want to learn how to dance or go traveling to the South Seas, utterly useless.

How valuable is money? It depends entirely on what we are trying to use it for.

Here are some of the most common things people attempt to use money for, along with a few of my thoughts on the relative value of money as a primary means to that end.

1. To get security

As we've seen in the example of the $600 million man, attempting to use money to get security is like trying to use a paperweight to hold down an 800-pound gorilla. It can seem as though it's working when the gorilla's not moving, but it's not really doing anything at all.

2. To get power and/or freedom

Any time we attempt to create an internal experience (power, freedom, etc.) through external means (accumulating a certain amount of money), we're bound to struggle because things simply don't work that way.

There is a famous story of Alexander the Great's encounter with the ascetic philosopher Diogenes. When Alexander asked Diogenes what he could do for him, Diogenes' only request was that Alexander step out of his sunlight so he could continue to enjoy the day. So impressed was Alexander by this encounter that he is reported to have said, 'Truly, were I not Alexander, I would have wished to be Diogenes.'

What did the most powerful man in the world admire about this poor philosopher who lived in a barrel (literally) by the side of a road? He was as free to live his life on his own terms as Alexander himself.

While it is certainly true that you can use your money to influence the actions of others, money cannot ultimately take away the ultimate power within each individual – what

Holocaust survivor Viktor Frankl called 'the last of the human freedoms – the freedom to choose.'

3. To save time

One of the interesting things I've learned from my wealthiest clients is that they don't value money nearly as much as they value time. While many people will spend hours and hours to try and save a few hundred dollars, the wealthy will happily spend hundreds of dollars to save a few hours of time.

4. To get stuff and/or experiences

As we've seen in my earlier definition, this is what money was actually designed for: to facilitate the exchange of goods and services. Using money to get experiences (like a great vacation or an amazing seminar) or stuff (like food, clothing, and shelter) is the equivalent of using a hammer to pound a nail.

Which nails in particular you choose to pound (and of course which experiences and stuff you choose to use your money for) is a function of the thinking you have that looks real to you and your attunement to your own inner sense of desire and joy.

5. To get more money

The comedian Jerry Seinfeld used to tell a joke about why he wasn't an investor:

> People always tell me, 'You should have your money
> working for you.' I've decided I'll do the work and let my
> money relax.

While many people in the current economy could find cause to agree with him, there is no question that one of the ways you know you have mastered money in your life is when a certain portion of your money is working to earn more money for you while you sit back and relax at home.

The only danger in getting too caught up in this investor mindset is that it's easy to lose sight of what the money is for – that is, *why* are you seeking to accumulate more money in the first place?

If it's for greater security, power, or freedom, well, as the disclaimer always says, 'The value of your investments can go down as well as up and cannot be guaranteed.'

If, on the other hand, it's to purchase a more diverse set of stuff and experiences for yourself and others and your experience of the creation is a joyous one, well, the more, the merrier.

6. To give hope, opportunity, and the chance of a better life

Most books I have read on charity or philanthropy talk about the value of giving of yourself, rather than of your money. While there is no doubt that giving of your time, energy, and attention can be a wonderful gift to both yourself and your community, what nobody ever talks about is how much fun it is to put your money to use, even if you don't yet have very much of it.

Each December when the kids were little, we would give them money with the instruction that they should find a way to use it that would create a better world for others. One year

14-year-old Oliver used his to support breast cancer research, 11-year-old Clara used hers to support a children's hospital, and six-year-old Maisy split hers between a charity that prevented cruelty to animals and one that built schools in impoverished areas, because she couldn't believe there were kids who didn't have the chance to go to school.

Over the years my family and I have given away as little as $10 to feed a hungry child and so much to one organization that they thought we were joking, but in both cases the fun we had doing it and the sense of contribution it engendered were the same.

So, whether you're struggling to make ends meet or pretending you don't have 10 years' worth of savings put by and need to continue to struggle, consider borrowing this line I wrote on the back of my checkbook nearly 20 years ago:

A portion of all I earn is mine to give away.

Which begs the question of how we make money in the first place…

HOW TO MAKE MONEY

'You don't get what you deserve in life – you get what you negotiate.'
CHESTER L. KARRASS

Economics is a vast and complex field, but in some ways it can be reduced to one simple principle:

> The scarcer the resource, the more people
> are willing to give up in order to get it; the
> more common the resource, the less people
> are willing to give up in order to get it.

That means that on the one hand, a plot of land in the heart of the city will nearly always fetch more than the same size plot in the country; on the other hand, no one would ever bribe the *maître d'* to get into a McDonald's.

Why do we put up with boorish behavior and ignorant decision-making from the people above us in our company? Why is the customer 'always right'? Because in both cases, they're the ones with the money, and we're seeing ourselves as a common resource in pursuit of a scarce one.

In order to turn that equation around, you simply need to see the abundance of money that surrounds you. Recent estimates place the wealth of the world at over $80 trillion. Yet the fundamental mistake that nearly everyone makes when it comes to wealth is to think of money as a scarce resource. But if there's over $80 trillion floating around and only one of you, how is *money* the scarce resource?

The point is this:

> As long as you see money as a
> scarce resource, you will continually
> inconvenience yourself in order to
> get it. As soon as you have made

yourself the scarce resource, money
will inconvenience itself to get you.

By way of example, a number of years ago Steve Chandler and I were running a money course and I got into a conversation with my then teenage son about what the people on the course were learning. When I told him that in one exercise I had given the group, the 18 participants had made over $84,000 between them in just one hour, he was gobsmacked.

'Do you mean in real money?' he asked. 'Is that even possible?'

When I assured him that I did indeed mean in 'real money,' he asked how they'd done it, and I outlined the three ways to make money that I am about to share with you. But I also pointed out that making money had not been the real point of the exercise.

What had been important had been bringing people's insecurities around making money to the surface in a fun and friendly atmosphere so they could look at them in the bright light of consciousness and see them for what they were – the energy of Thought taking form.

Each time we recognize the principle of Thought as the source of feeling, something seems to open up inside us and we feel our way through to the space of possibility on the far side of our thinking. And when there is no fear (i.e. 'fearlessness'), creativity, joy, and fun are the inevitable result.

While my son thought that was very 'coachy' of me, he still seemed curious about the three ways to make money, so I shared a bit about what had happened with the group. How had they made all that money in such a short space of time?

1. Planting Seeds

Many people seem to think of the game of sales as like putting coins into a slot machine – you make your offerings (put in your coins) and if you get lucky, sometimes the machine pays out. If it doesn't, you either keep putting in more coins in hopes of 'hitting the jackpot,' or you move on to another machine.

But when you approach sales from a place of joyful service, you realize that making offers is more like planting a garden than gambling. It's not about mechanics, it's about people. Instead of dropping coins into a machine, you're working with a living system. And instead of focusing on what you might get back if you're lucky, you take some time to think about what you'd like to grow. Plant a tomato seed and if it takes root, you'll wind up with a tomato plant. If you don't like tomatoes … well, that might not be your best plan!

Ask yourself questions like:

♦ What's in my heart that I would love to share with the world?

♦ Who would I love to impact, serve, or contribute to? What difference would I love to make for them?

♦ What would be the most powerful, fun, and useful thing I could do for this client or customer?

♦ If I dedicated my life to making this person/company's life better, what is the biggest difference I could make for them in the smallest amount of time?

When service-oriented 'difference-making' questions are asked from a place of joyful inquiry, the answers are inevitably creative, fun, and bring the seeds of opportunity with them.

2. Picking Fruit

Some of the largest financial gains people made in the hour were by going to existing clients and customers and creating wonderful offers designed especially for them. Since they already had a pre-existing service-based relationship with these people, they didn't have to 'water the soil' by establishing their credibility and ability to add value – they just had to find the differences they would love to make and the form in which they would most like to make them.

When the 'fruit was ripe' – i.e. there was a real fit between the offer and the person and the timing was right – the deals could be done on the spot.

How did they know the fruit was ripe? By reaching out, asking questions, and sharing from their true nature – that place of wellbeing that would be unaffected by either a 'yes' or a 'no.'

3. Exchanging Chickens

As we've already discussed, money was originally created as a means of exchange that would simplify the barter process.

Instead of having to carry chickens around with me that I could trade for baked goods or clothing or shelter, I could sell them for money and use the money to get the cupcake, sweater, or house.

So now, once I identify 'my chickens,' i.e. those goods or services I would love to offer that would make a positive difference to the lives of others, I can exchange them directly for cash.

How do you identify your 'chickens'? They meet at least one of two criteria:

1. You enjoy doing or creating them and do/create them really well.

2. Other people value receiving/using them.

So, your 'chicken' might be:

♦ Making cars run better or making homes immaculately clean.

♦ Facilitating the exchange of goods and services (i.e. 'sales') or facilitating the appreciation of beauty and wonder (i.e. 'art').

♦ The ability to design a rocket ship or kick a ball into a net.

After I had shared those ideas with my son and given him examples of what people had actually done, he asked me to explain the 'coachy' bit to him again. What was it that freed people up to access the kind of energy, creativity and fearlessness that led to all that money being made?

There are many ways to answer that question, but perhaps the simplest is this:

> *When you can clearly see the difference between what*
> *money is good for (i.e. facilitating the exchange of goods*
> *and services) and what money is terrible at (i.e. creating*
> *security, peace of mind, and happiness), you stop trying to*
> *make money to make yourself feel better and realize that*
> *the better you feel, the easier it is to make money.*

And when you begin to see that good feeling is part of your essential nature and not something that can ever be truly impacted by how much or how little you have, the game of money becomes considerably easier to play.

Supercoaching Tip
$100 in Your Pocket

Here's a question that I taught my friend Paul McKenna, a version of which he included in his wonderful book *I Can Make You Rich*:

> *If you woke up one morning in a place where you knew*
> *no one, with $100 in your pocket, how long would it take*
> *you to double your money and how would you do it?*

Once you've answered that question, how long would it take you to double it again, and how would you do it? And again? And again?

The more answers you can come up with, the more your financial future is secured. If you think you've run out of ideas, reflect on these words attributed to Thomas Edison: 'When you have exhausted all possibilities, remember this – you haven't.'

THE INVISIBLE OBSTACLE TO WEALTH

'The lack of money is the root of all evil.'
MARK TWAIN

As with any other creation, creating money is essentially a very simple process:

1. Aim yourself in a direction.

2. Show up and respond to what shows up.

If you really want to create money, the only thing that can stop you is a thought believed. And the thought that more than any other seems to separate the haves from the have-nots – or at least the 'have-mores' from the 'have-lesses' – is so subtle that it's nearly invisible.

I remember when one of my coaches first pointed out that the biggest obstacle to my own wealth was my belief that I needed the money. We reviewed a number of my business dealings over the years, and one by one he pointed out how I'd settled for less than I wanted because I'd thought I had to take whatever was on offer. To my surprise, we also noticed several situations where I'd blown it because my desperate sense of need had been driving me to try to squeeze every last penny out of every deal.

After that, each time I argued that I really did need the money, he would calmly ask me some variation on the question: 'What would happen if you didn't get it?' No matter how urgent or important each financial opportunity felt at the time, I would eventually realize that there was always another way forward and that no one opportunity was the be-all and end-all of my financial success.

Now, one of the first questions I ask my own clients if they have money concerns is this: 'How many days forward could you go without earning any money before you would be out on the street?'

To their own surprise, the answer is generally measured in years, not months or weeks. (Actually, the most common answer is: 'I would never be out on the street, because my family/friends/ community would make sure I had a place to stay until I got back on my feet.')

One client who had been arguing for his 'need' for money sheepishly admitted that he could go 10 years without working before running out of money. Based on this, we created an experiment. For the next three years, he would proceed in business from the assumption that he didn't need the money. All of his choices over that time period would be based on inspiration and true heartfelt desire. In other words, he was going to begin to do what he wanted to do, not what he thought he 'should' do or 'needed' to do. (We figured that would still give him seven years to go back to doing things out of desperation before he ran out of money!)

Although he struggled with it for several months, before the first year was out he had made more than 10 times as much money as he had the year before and was doing work that he really loved and wanted to do.

So how is it that by letting go of neediness he was able to create so much more wealth in his life? And more important, why would someone who clearly didn't need the money continue to act for all the world as if he did?

Let's take a look at each of these questions in turn.

Why Do You Make More Money When You Stop Needing It?

There are essentially three motivations for anything and everything we do: desperation, rationalization, and inspiration. In linguistic terms, these usually are expressed in terms of:

- ◆ 'I'm doing it because I have to' (desperation).

- ◆ 'I'm doing it because I should' (rationalization).

- ◆ 'I'm doing it because I want to' (inspiration).

When you act out of a sense of desperation (that is, neediness), you have to settle for whatever is on offer. There's generally a sense of urgency that shifts the balance in any negotiation in the other person's favor. What's more, you feel so uncomfortable in your own skin that you put your worst foot forward, trying too hard to please or shifting to the other side and putting on a front of anger or bravado to cover up your fear.

However, when you know that you don't need the money (because almost invariably, no matter what your fear has been telling you, you don't), you move forward with a sense of ease and wellbeing. It's easy to stick to your bottom line because you always have an alternative – getting on with your wonderful life and offering your creativity and skills at difference-making and value creation to any of the hundreds, thousands, and sometimes millions of people who would benefit from them.

You enter negotiations without fear, because whether or not you reach agreement, you know at an absolutely fundamental level that your wellbeing is not dependent on making a deal. And as we explored in Session Eight, when you're okay with the other person saying 'no,' you can ask for anything you want.

Stuart Wilde used to regale us for hours with stories of gas-station attendants who would attract customers from miles around with their five-star-hotel-quality toilets, or purveyors of knick-knacks who made hundreds of thousands of dollars from people who wanted to 'take home a little piece of the store.'

His point was always to begin your quest for wealth by working on yourself – seeing through your thoughts of neediness to your innate wellbeing. 'As you become more and more skilled at making a difference and happier and happier in yourself,' he would say, 'people will be drawn to you. They will want to spend time hanging out in your energy. And when they show up, bill 'em!'

'If I Don't Need the Money, Why Do I Feel So Needy?'

When it comes to money, nearly all of us have learned to motivate ourselves by creating feelings of worry, fear, and even desperation. 'If I can just stay scared enough,' this internal logic tells us, 'I'll be safe and I'll keep moving forward.' The problem with this point of view is that fear is one of the least effective states to move forward in – it impairs your reasoning, limits your vision, destroys your health, and gives off a horrible stench that puts people off doing business with you: the sickly smell of desperation.

(Think about it for a moment – who would you rather have working with you on a project? Someone who's inspired to make things happen or someone who's desperate not to mess things up?)

It's at this point in the discussion that someone inevitably says to me, 'That's all right for all your wealthy clients, but what if I really do need the money?'

Listen, if your children are starving or you're going to lose your apartment or house at the end of the month because you're six months in arrears on the rent or mortgage, do what you need to do to take care of yourself and your family.

But when I push them on it, nearly everyone who seems in dire straits could in reality go on for another three to six months by making a few adjustments to their lifestyle. And three to six months is more than enough time to put your creativity and inspiration to work on creating value, making a difference, and exchanging that value and difference-making for money.

Here's an exercise that might prove helpful:

Don't Need the Money

- Review all of your recent business dealings – contract negotiations, proposals, sales calls, or whatever else you do to make money. How much of your motivation was inspiration (doing it because you wanted to), how much rationalization (doing it because you felt you should), and how much was desperation (doing it because you thought you needed to)?

- Choose one business deal that you don't mind losing. If you don't have any deals pending, make one up – create a proposal that's so outlandish that you would love it if it came through, but you really don't need it to, because it's so 'out there.' Notice the difference in your own levels of engagement and creativity as you do so.

- Begin to say 'no' to things you don't want to do by asking for more money. If you really don't want to do them, ask for what seems to you to be a ridiculous amount of money. This will begin to establish a new pattern in your brain of asking for what you want without a sense of neediness. For example, I had the chance to work with the CEO of an international corporation on her presentation skills. While I wouldn't have minded the work, I wasn't terribly interested in it. Rather than turn it down, I created a six-figure coaching proposal – about four or five times the going rate at the time. I was pretty sure she'd reject the proposal, but if she had agreed, I would have happily completed the job.

  One word of warning: occasionally, people will say 'yes' to these outrageous proposals, so don't make them if you're truly unwilling to honor your end of the agreement!

Supercoaching Tip
'How Much Should I Charge?'

Some people think the limit on what they can charge has to do with their self-worth, but in fact it simply has to do with what they're willing to ask for. You'll almost never be paid more than you ask for, regardless of how much or how little you happen to believe you're worth.

I've found that most people I work with have a number in their head that can be accessed with a little prodding. So, if you (or someone you know) aren't sure what to charge for something, play the 'higher/lower' game:

1. Choose any number to start and ask, 'Is it [this number]?'

2. The only three acceptable answers are 'Higher,' 'Lower,' or 'That's it!'

3. Keep going until you've determined the perfect price for you.

What's great about this is that you never have to worry about getting it wrong. If it's too much, the marketplace will tell you by not giving you as much business as you want; if it's too little, you'll know because you'll be swamped!

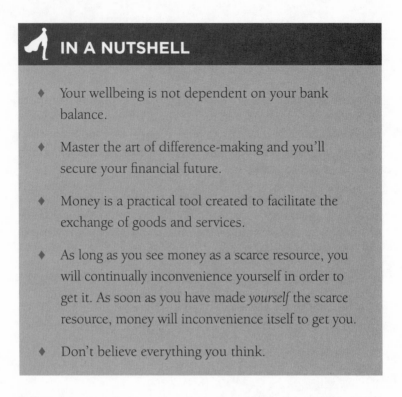

IN A NUTSHELL

♦ Your wellbeing is not dependent on your bank balance.

♦ Master the art of difference-making and you'll secure your financial future.

♦ Money is a practical tool created to facilitate the exchange of goods and services.

♦ As long as you see money as a scarce resource, you will continually inconvenience yourself in order to get it. As soon as you have made *yourself* the scarce resource, money will inconvenience itself to get you.

♦ Don't believe everything you think.

We're almost done! Feel free to reread this chapter or go back through any of the sessions and secrets we've covered up until now.

When you're ready, let's do one final session together...

Session Ten

THE POWER
OF HOPE

*'All dreams appear impossible until
someone makes them happen.'*
Barry Neil Kaufman

GOING UPSTREAM

A man was walking through a dark forest when he came to the bank of a huge river. As he marveled at the beauty and grandeur of the river, his attention was caught by something that sounded like a cry for help. Sure enough, he noticed someone drowning in the flow of the river, and he immediately waded in to rescue them.

The person he rescued was, of course, deeply grateful, and the man basked in the feeling of having contributed to life until he heard another cry for help and once again waded into the river and saved someone from drowning.

Each time he heard a cry for help he waded in; each time he saved someone, his good feeling was interrupted by another cry for help.

After a time, he grew lonely in his endeavor and he recruited some of those he had helped in rescuing the seemingly endless supply of people who were drowning in the flow of the river. Some did not feel capable, and some apologetically said they were too busy, but others stayed on until a community of helpers began to form.

They formed a village and elected the man their leader, for they saw him to be experienced, strong, compassionate, and wise.

And even though there were many more people drowning in the river than they could ever possibly save, they did their best with one and all.

Then one day, to the shock and horror of his followers, the man threw his hands up in the air and exclaimed, 'I've had enough of this! There are too many people drowning and not enough of us to help save them!' Without even a backward glance, he turned his back on the river and walked away.

Although they felt discouraged, the remaining helpers threw themselves back into their work with even more vigor, doing their best to save each person they could, even while knowing that for every one they pulled out of the river, three more would float on by.

'Made a difference to that one,' they would say, reminding themselves of the woman who spent her days throwing starfish back into the ocean that had washed up on the shore.

One morning they woke to find the river flowing in all its majesty, but not a single cry for help. It seemed a blessed day, and they promised themselves and one another that they would never forget it for the rest of their lives. But there was even more to come.

Every day that followed, the helpers went to the river to save the drowning, and each day came and went without a single incident.

Then one day something truly remarkable happened. There were once again people in the river, but when the helpers waded out to save them, the people in the river laughed.

'We're not drowning, we're waving!' they said.

Later that day, their former leader appeared at the village by the side of the river, returning as if he hadn't a care in the world. Many were happy to see him, but some were still angry at what they viewed as his betrayal and abandonment.

'Why did you leave us?' they asked. 'Why did you abandon the cause?'

'I never abandoned you, my friends,' the man replied. 'I simply went upstream to stop people from falling in and to teach them how to swim.'

THE 10TH SECRET

I was teaching a seminar a number of years ago when a woman stood up, dripping with disgust, and pointed an accusatory finger at me. 'The problem with you,' she said, 'is that you give people hope.'

She had a point, although in my defense it had never occurred to me that this might be perceived as a bad thing. But she was also inaccurate in her description. I can't 'give' anyone hope any more than I can give them anger or fear. What I can do, and do whenever I can, is point to a deeper understanding of where hope comes from and why it's such a wonderful thing when it comes.

I've actually often wondered when hope got such a bad name. Criticism of both classical religion and New Age thinking is filled with accusations of giving people 'false hope.' But what makes hope false?

The Oxford American Dictionary defines 'hope' as 'a feeling of expectation and desire for a certain thing to happen' and as 'grounds for believing that something good may happen.' False hope, then, doesn't have to do with my feeling of expectation and desire for my relationships to be successful, my business to make money, and my body to recover from an illness, but with my grounds for believing that these things are possible.

If I ask you to double down on your dreams because I have 'secret' knowledge of the future that reveals that as long as you do X, Y, and Z, you'll ultimately succeed, that is unfortunately false grounds for hope – I have no such knowledge. However, if I ask you to move forward on your dreams because there are hundreds of thousands of stories of people who have succeeded in spite of the odds, no matter how heavily those odds have seemed stacked against them, that is indeed legitimate grounds for hope, regardless of how things ultimately turn out.

(A quick aside about 'evidence': in days gone by, evidence has clearly 'proven' that the sun revolves around the Earth, which is in fact flat; that bumblebees can't fly; and that humankind will not only never reach the moon, but can't run a mile in less than four minutes or find true and lasting happiness in a world filled with suffering – oh, wait, is that one still a fact?!)

Here's my definition of hope:

> *Hope is the magic elixir that energizes dreams, fuels possibilities, and lets you live beyond the limits of your habitual thinking. It's not a promise that something you want will happen – it's an invitation to enjoy the possibility of what you want while you and life negotiate the eventual outcome.*

And here's our 10th and final secret:

Hope is the gateway to new possibilities.

In *The Lord of the Rings* trilogy, J.R.R. Tolkien equates 'good magic' with awakening hope and 'dark magic' with covering it over. In my work with clients, I find the same thing to be true. Until they uncover hopeful thinking, there's no spark in their eyes or spring in their step. Once that hopeful feeling is awakened, everything becomes possible.

How Do You Awaken Hope?

1. Stop arguing for why you can't have what you want

For a number of years, I worked alongside Dr Richard Bandler. He had a simple dictum he brought out whenever someone started making the case for their own limitations:

If you can't, you won't.

As someone who loves to use three words when one would probably do, my preferred version is this:

Whether you think you can or you think you can't, you don't actually know, so why limit yourself by guessing?

If instead of arguing for your limitations you argue for your possibilities, you will find much more capacity and creativity inside you than you ever dreamed possible.

What if your dream could happen? Yes, I know, but what if it could? What then?

2. Check in to see if you actually want it

A friend told me that before she died, Syd Banks' first wife, Barb, said, 'You can have anything you want – you just have to actually want it.' This was, in fact, the point at the heart of my first book. No matter how hard you try, it's really difficult to keep yourself moving forward long enough to create what you don't actually want in the first place.

How do you know what you *do* want? While it's something that you'll get a feel for over time, a simple way to check is to ask yourself, 'If this fell into my lap out of a clear blue sky, would I take it?'

If your answer is anything other than an emphatic and obvious 'yes,' move on.

3. Take the first step

One of my favorite bits of 'wisdom fiction' is Ken Roberts' book *A Rich Man's Secret*. On a mysterious tombstone, the young seeker at the heart of the story sees the following phrase engraved in marble:

> *Take the first step, no more, no less, and the next will be revealed.*

It sounds easy, but I've found that people have so many good reasons not to move forward on their dreams that their creativity shuts down and they literally can't see what's possible. They make up the future and then decide what to do or not do based on what they've made up.

Here's a simple truth I've seen play itself out again and again in my life and the lives of my clients:

> You can't think your way out of a problem you've made up with your thinking.

If you know you want to head in a particular direction, take the first step. In my experience, you'll not only be pleasantly surprised by where you end up, you'll be even more pleasantly surprised by how quickly you get there.

WHAT'S THEIR DREAM?

'The greatest good we can do for others is not just to share our riches with them, but to reveal theirs.'
Zig Ziglar

In his book *The Dream Manager*, Matthew Kelly tells the story of a large cleaning company that solved the problem of high employee turnover by hiring a 'dream manager' – in essence an in-house life coach whose job it was to help people articulate their dreams, formulate plans, and follow them through to achievement.

Along the way, he raises an interesting question:

How well do you know the dreams of the people closest to you?

When I first read the book many years ago, I assumed my answer would be: 'Really, really well indeed.' But rather than trust my assessment, I decided to actually find out.

First up was my wife. Although I was embarrassed to ask (after all, surely I should know what the woman I love's heart longs for), I was heartened by her clarity about her dreams for us as a family and a few personal ones, but I could hear her hesitancy about realizing them. It was then that I realized that one of the most profound ways I could support her was by working with her on making her dreams come true instead of acting as a 'devil's advocate' against them. (A complete aside, but does the devil really need an advocate? And if so, is that really whom you want as your employer?)

Next were the kids. Oliver dreamed of life in high school and saving up for a Ford Mustang as his first car. Clara wanted to sing and act, and Maisy was dead set on becoming a mermaid and then going to medical school.

While life has moved on and their dreams have grown and changed, their willingness to dream and the discovery that it's possible to make your dreams come true has turned them into what T. E. Lawrence called 'dreamers of the day.' As he said in his autobiography:

> All men dream: but not all equally. Those who dream by night in the dusty recesses of their minds wake in the day to find that it was all vanity: but the dreamers of the day are dangerous . . . for they may act their dream with open eyes, to make it possible.

And that's what I want for everyone in my life – my family, my friends, my clients – and yes, even you: that you may act your dreams with open eyes and make them possible.

Supercoaching Tip
What's Their Dream?

I think you'll be surprised by how much you enjoy this little experiment...

1.   Make a list of the three to five most important people in your life.

2. Take some time this week to ask them about their dreams – what they long for, what they would love, and what would make them go 'Wow!'

3. Let them know you're on their side – that you love them, believe in them, and will support and assist them in making their dreams come true.

4. Ask at least three people you don't know well (or even at all!) what their dreams are for their lives.

While not everyone is up for this conversation, the connection you make with the ones who are will make a tremendous difference in your own sense of joy and meaning in your life.

HOPE FOR HUMANITY

'Argue for your limitations, and sure enough, they're yours.'

RICHARD BACH

I had a client once who spent the first two days of a three-day coaching intensive arguing with me about all the very real reasons why his life was awful and was sure to get even worse going forward. Any alternative possibility I presented was quickly shot down by an additional set of facts about the past or projections about the future.

By the end of the second day, somewhat exasperated, I said to him, 'I can tell you right now I see the possibility of a bright future for you, and I know for a fact you could be enjoying your life right now, today, in this moment, regardless of what's going on. And you'd better hope that I'm right and you're wrong.

Because if you're right, you're screwed; if I'm right, at least there's the possibility of better times ahead.'

Surprised and a bit taken aback by my outburst, he asked me what I thought he should do.

'You're going to have to find a way to shut the hell up in your mind,' I said, 'and listen for something new – something you don't already think and something you don't already "know." If you do, I promise you you'll hear something that will change this for you.'

To his credit, he did, and he was like a different person by the time he left at the end of the next day. His only complaint was that I hadn't told him to 'shut up' early enough in our time together.

Now I don't know what's going on in the world at the time you're reading this, but it's a pretty safe bet that there are some things going on that you wish weren't happening, that you're thinking lots of thoughts about how horrible things are going to be in the future because of it, and that you're feeling that horrible thinking as though those things are already happening now.

It's an equally safe bet that there are some people in the world who are either happy or indifferent about those same things, and they're either thinking lots of thoughts about how wonderful things are going to be in the future or not thinking much of anything at this moment.

That's just how the mind works – we live in the feeling of our 'right now' thinking, moment by moment by moment.

To the extent that we know that, we have a bit of space around it – we don't have to take it to heart and project it out into the future. If it looks to us as though our feelings are coming from the outside world, we'll be stuck in them – and things will not only look bad now, they'll look as though they've always been bad and will only get worse.

One of my students recently likened this to waking up with a terrible hangover. If she hadn't understood the nature of hangovers, she told me, she would have genuinely thought she was dying. She might have taken the time to get her affairs in order, done her best to make peace with her unresolved conflicts, and called an ambulance to take her to the hospital. But because she knew how hangovers worked, she took a couple of aspirin, promised herself that she would never drink that much again (with her fingers crossed behind her back, obviously), and got on with her day, knowing that hangovers go away all by themselves as the amazing self-correcting mechanism of the body brings itself back to a healthy equilibrium.

Similarly, if we understand the nature of the mind, we know that when we feel miserable, bleak, and hopeless, it's because we're caught up in some miserable, bleak, and hopeless thinking. And we also know that the moment we put that thinking to one side, the amazing self-correcting mechanism of the mind will bring us some fresh new thinking and creative, hopeful possibilities as it brings itself back to a healthy equilibrium.

But how do we do it? How do we put down our thinking when everything in us is telling us we need to take things more seriously, not less? How do we allow our natural buoyancy and resilience to come to the surface when the problem seems so much more deeply rooted than something as frivolous as 'a passing thought'?

I can only share what helps me; hopefully you'll find something in it that triggers your own natural capacity for insight, creativity, and realization...

Stop Saying 'It's Just a Thought'

In 2013, I decided to take a year off from running Supercoach Academy until I could find a better way of sharing the three principles at the heart of my work.

I'd noticed that the most frequent thing I heard students and clients saying was 'I know it's just a thought, but...' and then finishing the sentence with things that indicated their problem was nothing to do with their thinking and everything to do with their past, future, and the world around them.

Here's the thing: saying 'It's just a thought' is like saying 'It's just nuclear energy.' Thought is the most powerful force in the universe, and while it can do a tremendous amount of good when handled with care and respect, it can destroy the world when misused or misunderstood.

If you've ever wanted to smack someone who's come up to you in the midst of a personal crisis and told you, 'It's just your thinking,' you'll know that the feelings we feel in response to our thoughts are 100 percent real in the body. They are not illusory and almost never feel temporary. The strength of those feelings gives you an indication of just how powerful thought really is.

It's when you see that the *only* source of those feelings is a passing thought – not the remembered past, not an imagined future, not even the most recent election results – the self-correcting mechanism of the mind kicks into action and your thoughts begin to change for the better.

See the Disconnect between Feeling Bad and Doing Good

Martin Luther King had a dream. Mother Teresa had a mission. Nelson Mandela had a vision. While the movements they inspired were forged in a cauldron of social inequality and unrest, their personal stories are filled with examples of their love for humanity and their hope for a positive future.

One of the reasons that people think they need to feel bad in order to make a change is that often our dreams and visions for a positive future come to us at seemingly low points in our lives, at times when we've been almost forced to go inside and take stock – to find out what we know to be true underneath the constant noise of our habitual thinking. This deeper knowing never comes with feelings of anger or fear. It carries with it a feeling of resolve, and of hope, and of love, and of peace. We may not know how things are going to change, but we know we will be an agent of that change and that it will be a positive one.

We don't need to stay angry to make a difference – in fact, it's one of the least efficient ways of doing so. Anger may get people to gather in the street, but it's inspiration that gets them to march forward instead of mobbing up and destroying whatever they see around them.

Where does that inspiration come from?

It comes from deep inside us, and it comes through in the moments that our constant thinking about how the world needs to change pauses. Then we find a little sliver of quiet – a space between thoughts – and through that space our path begins to emerge.

As Marianne Williamson said, 'God heard us. He sent help. He sent you.'

Open Your Mind to New Possibilities

Have you ever wondered how it's possible that seemingly intelligent people disagree with you?

One explanation is that they're just a bit confused, and when they come to their senses, they'll agree with you. Another is that they're not as intelligent as you thought they were. A third, and in my mind more accurate explanation, is that we all live in separate realities.

We think the mind works like a camera, accurately recording what's really going on around it, but in actuality, the mind works more like a projector. It projects our thoughts onto the screen of our consciousness, and then we experience that created world through our senses.

That's why nearly everyone who looks at this image sees an upside-down white triangle that's bold in the middle:

In truth, there are no triangles or circles at all in the image – just a series of lines and shapes on a field of white space. Our minds fill in that space, projecting an illusory upside-down triangle on top of three made-up circles and a 'right-side up' triangle that everyone can see but only exists in our imagination.

We have no way of knowing what's 'actually' going on in some imagined real world – we can only take in the second-hand smoke of our own thinking. And that means we're all living in separate realities. Not separate interpretations of a 'real' reality, but seven billion individual overlapping creations.

Which is why someone can apparently look at the same things we're looking at and come to different conclusions. We're not *actually* looking at the same thing. They're looking at their own thought-created reality; we're looking at ours. We're both absolutely right, given what we see, but our perception of what's going on is absolutely limited. As Syd Banks said and I've repeated several times throughout this book, 'Everyone is doing the best they can, given the thinking they have that looks real to them.'

So you can't change someone's mind without first opening up your own. What do they see that you don't? What babies of wisdom and truth are you throwing out in the bathwater of their rhetoric?

We can absolutely learn from one another and we can become partners in creating a better world by striving to see what others see. In a podcast called *How to Become More Intelligent, Beginning Today* (www.michaelneill.org/supercoach), I shared what I consider to be a master strategy for increasing your intelligence and becoming more influential with others:

> *Find someone you recognize to not be a complete moron*
> *who disagrees with you and really listen to them.*

Don't worry about all the people who disagree with you because of their ignorance or hidden agendas. They're out there too. Don't worry about getting your point of view across. You'll be able to do that more powerfully once you recognize that it's just a point of view. But find one person who might see something you don't and learn what you can learn from them. Repeat it as often as you can. Be the change you wish to see in the world.

Supercoaching Tip
Changing the World, One Person at a Time

1. Choose a person in your life whom you deeply love and would love to see tap into the power within them.

2. When you next spend time with them, decide to be with them as they are, without trying to change, fix, or help them in any way. Know in your heart that no matter what

is going on, they have the ability at any moment to spread their wings and go from falling to flying.

3. Do the same thing with yourself and see what happens!

THE BEGINNER'S GUIDE TO SHARING THE THREE PRINCIPLES

I began this session with a quote from Richard Bach's wonderful book *Illusions*: 'Argue for your limitations, and sure enough, they're yours.' I'll put it somewhat less poetically here, but hopefully with equal strength:

> *Argue for your possibilities, and sure enough, you'll find much more capacity and ability inside yourself than you ever dreamed possible.*

I hope that by this point in our time together you've begun to see that you're far more than your thinking, and that your potential to impact the world is effectively beyond your imagination. So I'd like to bring this session and indeed our time together to a close with an invitation – the invitation to live with hope, with the awareness that we're all more capable than we think.

There's no movement to join, no manifesto to sign, just a gentle reminder and an open invitation to be the difference-maker in someone else's life and to be open to having that difference made in your own. Tell someone you see the potential in them. Mean it. Demonstrate it in the way you treat them. Then stand back and watch their life begin to blossom and bloom.

If you'd like to share the three principles with others, here are a few phrases that one of our Supercoach Academy graduates, Nikki Welch, used to sum up the potential impact of this understanding on the way we help others and live our lives:

'Oh well...'

My friend Cathy Casey is a kind of 'inmate whisperer' who has used her understanding of the three principles to help countless people in the prison system reconnect with their innate wisdom and wellbeing and, where possible, reintegrate with society after their incarceration with a remarkably low rate of recidivism.

She has told me on many occasions of the startling realization that many of the prisoners had when they first began to see that experience comes via Thought, not from other people or circumstances in the world.

'Had I known then what I know now,' they would say with regret and sometimes horror, 'I wouldn't have done what I did.'

'Oh well,' Cathy would say, eyebrows arched in both acceptance and recognition of the fact that recognizing innocence and accepting consequences are not mutually exclusive.

For myself, I first really got this when I was beating myself up for all the suffering I put myself through as I did my best to cope with years of depression and suicidal ideation that I never dreamed were the result of a simple misunderstanding of where my feelings and experience actually came from.

The principles-based psychiatrist William Pettit asked me to consider that no matter how long someone has been stumbling around in the dark, when the lights come on, they have two choices. They can beat themselves up for the damage they did when it was dark, or they can be grateful for the light. Since that day, with each new insight I have into how things really work and how much more gracefully I am able to handle life when I see the invisible energies behind it, I have done my best to say 'Oh well,' make amends where I can, and gratefully move forward with a higher level of understanding and compassion than before.

Which brings us to phrase two…

'Me too!'

There is a myth that seems common to pretty much everybody who learns about the nature of Mind, Consciousness, and Thought that when they *really* understand how things work, they'll never be unhappy, make mistakes, or struggle ever again. Which is a bit like expecting studying gravity to make you immune to its effects. Unlike Wile E. Coyote in every Road Runner cartoon ever, gravity pulls us toward the ground long before we think to look down and see how far we have to fall.

These principles are fully explanatory and highly predictive because they're in play whether we know about them, like them, or believe in them. Which means that all of us who study them tend to have a lot of compassion for the suffering of others. Like them, we get caught up in our thoughts from time to time. And like them, when we do, we're prone to stress, pressure, insecurity, and all the other feelings that come with the illusion that our feelings are coming at us from the outside world instead of from the invisible energy of Thought taking form inside us.

So while we may not take our suffering to heart in the same way, knowing that Thought is a transient energy that ebbs and flows on its own without needing or benefitting from our intervention, we still fall for the illusion and feel it just the same.

In fact, every time I'm starting to feel proud of how much my understanding of these principles is helping me cope with truly difficult circumstances, I get caught out. Because at some point it becomes apparent to me that it's not my depth of understanding that's helping me cope; it's my lack of understanding that's making it look as though there's something outside me I need to cope with.

Fortunately, we have phrase three:

'Next!'

Mara Olsen, the co-founder of the One Solution Global Initiative and one of my daughter's favorite human beings on the planet, was sharing a story at a recent training about the first time she had to present the principles to what she perceived to be a 'hostile' audience. Each time she started to go down a rabbit hole of self-doubt, she recognized that those thoughts weren't going to take her anywhere useful and heard a voice inside her own head call out, 'Next!' and call forth something fresh, like going back to the drawing board and starting a new page instead of desperately trying to fix the old one.

We are innately resilient because there are an infinite number of blank pages in the universe, and this capacity for fresh thought is one of the most hopeful implications of the principles. We are naturally creative because we're not stuck with our habitual thinking, no matter how many years we've been thinking it. We don't even have to find a better way – we can just let go of what we know doesn't work and make space for something better to come along. And because of the infinite creative potential of the deeper mind, something better inevitably will.

Which brings us to a fourth phrase, my own personal favorite, one that I hear myself saying more than any other in my coaching and teaching...

'No, really!'

There was a lovely moment on one of our programs when one of the participants was sharing his anxiety about going out into the world and actually speaking to people about what was possible for them without having any tools or techniques to hold on to. When the person coaching him gently asked him where he thought that experience of anxiety was coming from, he seemed confused. Then his eyes lit up.

'Do you mean that this isn't just a positive philosophy? I'm *actually* feeling Thought in the moment, not the stress of a future challenge?'

In that one moment of insight, his level of consciousness shifted and his experience of his experience changed. Instead of looking like the natural result of trying something new, his anxiety now looked like what it was: the feeling of thinking anxiously about an imaginary future.

Since thinking anxiously about an imaginary future didn't seem like a good idea to him, he was willing to let that thinking pass through, and, as inevitably happens, new thoughts came along that inspired him and took his experience in a different and more helpful direction.

So, if you're wondering whether or not this will 'work' for you, all I can tell you is to look for yourself and see what you can see. And if you get stuck, don't really get it, or are beating yourself up for all the things you would have done differently had you understood this earlier...

Oh well.

Me too.

Next!

(No, really...!)

IN A NUTSHELL

- Hope is the gateway to new possibilities. It isn't a promise that something you want will happen; it's an invitation to enjoy the possibility of what you want while you and life negotiate the eventual outcome.

- There is *never* a good reason not to hope.

- You can't think your way out of a problem you've made up with your thinking.

- Oh well... Me too. Next! (No, really...)

ARE YOU READY TO BECOME A SUPERCOACH?

'When you were born, you cried and the world rejoiced. Live your life in such a way that when you die, the world cries and you rejoice.'

Indian proverb

THE BODHISATTVA'S VOW

One day, a seeker who had devoted many lifetimes to attaining enlightenment broke through the habitual thinking of his everyday mind and saw the world around him as no more than *samsara*, a projection of his own largely fearful thoughts. His entire being was filled with joy, and he felt as if every cell in his body was dissolving into the bliss of *nirvana*. It was as though the gates of heaven had opened up to him and he glided effortlessly toward them.

But no sooner had he set one foot in heaven than he heard a sound that filled his heart with compassion. He turned back to see a seemingly infinite number of perfect beings acting for all the world like trapped cattle, struggling to make their way in the world and suffering at the hands of phantoms created by their own thoughts.

In that moment, he made this vow: 'For as long as space endures, and for as long as living beings remain, until then may I too abide to dispel the misery of the world.'

To this day, it is said, the Bodhisattva works tirelessly for the liberation of all sentient beings, one foot planted firmly in heaven, the other planted firmly here on Earth.

THE THREE STAGES OF UNDERSTANDING

Here are the 10 hidden truths we've been exploring in this book:

1. Your world is what you think it is, but there's a world beyond your thinking.

2. Wellbeing is not the fruit of something you do; it's the essence of who you are. There is nothing you need to change, do, be, or have in order to be happy.

3. There's nowhere for you to get to – you're already *here*.

4. There's no such thing as a decision – you either know what to do or you don't.

5. Every feeling you experience is the shadow of a thought, not a reflection of the world around you. You're living in the feeling of your thinking, not the feeling of your circumstances.

6. You have an innate, real-time responsive intelligence you can rely on to let you know what to do when it's time to do it.

7. Connection is what happens when human beings spend time together without their thinking getting in the way.

8. You can ask anyone for anything if you don't buy into your thinking about what it would mean if they said 'no.'

9. Your wellbeing is not dependent on your bank balance. Master the art of difference-making and you secure your financial future.

10. Hope is the gateway to new possibilities.

As you begin to gain insight into these truths and the principles behind them, your life will begin to transform. Results will matter less than ever, and you'll find yourself producing them even more consistently. Your fears and stresses will fall away as you recognize that they are made of the same gift of Thought that allows you to experience miracles in the world. While everyone's insights are unique and personal to them, I find there are some fairly consistent stages of understanding people go through as they dive deeper into the inside-out nature of experience...

Stage 1: Shifting the foundations

The general report from people when they gain their first insights into Mind, Thought, and Consciousness is that a sense of ease and wellbeing begins to permeate their lives, coupled with a sense of surprise that things have begun to shift in their circumstances 'all by themselves.' This can be unsettling. As one client said to me with great concern in his voice, 'The problem is, I don't have any more problems.'

When you're at this stage, you may find yourself worrying about not being worried, and being a bit upset about the fact that nothing seems to upset you anymore. As another client told me, 'It feels as though something is missing from my life.' When we explored this further, it turned out that what was missing was all the stress he was used to experiencing.

While for some people the relief of reaching this kind of equanimity is more than enough, I'm equally interested in what becomes possible because of it. Some of my clients were already pretty far down the road to success when they first hired me, but after a while it's as though they've learned a whole new way of being in the world. That's why for me peace of mind and greater contentment and happiness are both 'the end of the road' and the path forward – the place where the journey really begins…

Stage 2: Experiencing Effortless Success

When people begin experiencing a more effortless way of living, the results they produce (and the way in which they produce them) can be quite startling. Customers and clients appear out of nowhere. Business opportunities show up 'out of the blue.' Relationship miracles occur and seemingly insurmountable problems simply dissolve without ever being addressed directly.

At this stage, people often go back and forth between being thrilled with the way that their lives are unfolding and terrified that 'the magic will stop working' and they'll go right back to how things were before they started.

One day a client explained this feeling to me by saying, 'It's like I'm driving my daddy's Ferrari – it's incredible fun, and I'm really moving forward, but every time I start to feel that I'm going too fast, I slam on the brakes because I'm terrified of crashing the car!'

My explanation for this is simple:

Traditional success models are all about doing; creating effortless success is all about being.

It's easy to track the cause and effect with a doing-based model – the more you do, the better the result. But when you're experiencing effortless success, you do less and achieve more.

People often get uncomfortable in this stage because they haven't yet seen the connection between how they're showing up on a daily basis and the results they're producing in the world. In some cases, the discomfort can get so, well, uncomfortable that people would rather go back to doing things the way they used to. Even though it's harder and less sustainable, at least it makes sense to them – at least they feel they have some control.

Also, amazing things happen at first, but the results begin to diminish over time. It seems as though things aren't working as well as they used to, or that the 'magic' only works on the small stuff.

But for the people who stick with it, there's a third stage – the most wonderful stage of all…

Stage 3: Living a miraculous life

At some point, people begin to understand that effortless success isn't magic (although it certainly is magical) – it's the natural result of approaching life from a place of profound wellbeing, listening for the inner call, and following it wherever it may lead.

At this stage, you realize it's not your daddy's Ferrari, it's yours – and it's just one of the wonderful cars you have in your garage. There's no fear that 'it will stop working' because you realize that 'it' has never worked – the power to create a life well-lived was inside you right from the very beginning.

When I was first learning to become a coach, my favorite stories were about the Taoist sages who used to wander from village to village in ancient China. Although these sages held a variety of jobs in a disparate array of professions, they lived in such harmony with themselves and the world around them that whenever they passed through a town, disputes would resolve themselves and problems would be 'dis-solved' in the clarity of their presence. Without necessarily working directly to help others, these sages were a healing power in the world.

As your life gets better and better, it will begin to have a positive impact on the people around you and transform their lives, too. Even if your job description isn't part of the helping profession, people will just feel more relaxed in themselves when they're with you. They'll find themselves experiencing more success in their lives and producing results far beyond their efforts. There is nothing you need to do to make this happen – it's the natural result of resting in your innate wellbeing and evolving in your understanding of how our experience is only ever being created from the inside out.

As your understanding of the three principles behind these 'secrets' deepens, you'll become like one of these ancient sages – or at least their modern equivalent: a supercoach! While this will bring you untold joys in your life, it will also bring an interesting new responsibility…

THE HELPER'S DILEMMA

*'But this is the most important rule to follow: always make
the differences you can make, not the differences you would
prefer to make but can't.'*
LYNDON DUKE

Once upon a time I used to walk out in front of a group to
deliver a talk or a workshop with the simple intention of sharing
the best of what I know, from my heart. If people had insights
and acted on what they saw, wonderful; if they didn't, 'no
harm, no foul.' But as the years have gone by and more and
more people have heard me speak and my books and blogs
and radio shows have brought me some measure of reputation
and authority, I notice that people are now willing to act on
what I say simply because I'm the one saying it. They're more
likely to bypass their own inner wisdom in favor of my clever
catechisms, using my words not as catalysts for their inspiration
but as temporary replacements. 'After all,' one seminar attendee
said to me, 'you're *you*, and I'm only me!'

This came to a head for me when I was speaking at the United
Nations to a small group of delegates, spouses, interns, and
friends. The talk was an exploration of cultural mythology and
how it impacts the global pursuit of success and happiness.
Afterward, as often happens, people came up to me seeking
guidance about situations in their personal and professional
lives, ranging from diplomatic issues to weight loss and child
rearing. But when one young person approached me to ask
whether I thought she should 'break free of cultural mythology'

and give up her virginity before marriage, I found myself face to face with every helper's dilemma:

> The more successful we become in our desire to make a positive difference in the world, the more capable we become of doing damage.

Do we press on with a willingness to follow the utilitarian philosophy of 'Kill one, save many'? Or do we mute ourselves, following the Hippocratic dictum 'First, do no harm'?

I'm a man of my time, so I get my inspiration as often from movies as I do from ancient philosophical treatises. And I've found my own resolution to this dilemma in the Frank Capra film *It's a Wonderful Life*. In it, Jimmy Stewart's character wishes he had never been born, and his wish is granted. An angel named Clarence guides him through a vision of the world where his voice has never been heard. And in the darkness of that vision, he becomes reacquainted with his light and the difference he was born to make in the lives of others.

So here's the best of what I know, from my heart:

♦ You have wisdom inside you – listen for it and give it voice.

♦ You have light inside you – feel its glow and let it shine.

♦ You have power inside you – let your wisdom and light guide you as you make a difference in the world.

With all my love,

Michael

ACKNOWLEDGMENTS

On my wedding day, a man I had never seen before came up to me and said, 'You owe me, you know. If it wasn't for me, your wife would never have been born.' To reassure me I wasn't stumbling across a dark family secret just moments after joining the family, he went on to tell me his story.

He had been traveling in rural England in the 1950s, and because his watch was running a bit slow, he missed his train. While waiting for the next train to arrive, he bumped into a young woman on the platform. They shared a carriage on that train, and a little over a year later decided to share their lives with each other.

Still not making the connection, I asked him what that had to do with Nina being born. He seemed surprised that I didn't get it. 'Well, if I hadn't missed my train, I would never have met my wife, and your wife's parents would never have met each other at our wedding!'

Although there are far more people who contributed to both editions of this manuscript than I could possibly acknowledge, including those whose contributions are somewhat obscured by the mists of time, I would like to offer my very public thanks to the following for their coaching and support over the early years of my coaching career: Richard Bandler, Martha Beck, Steve Chandler, Michele Christensen, Steve Hardison, Kim Hare, Robert Holden, John La Valle, Jen Louden, Jay Perry, John Seymour, and Stuart Wilde.

In addition, my deepest gratitude goes to:

♦ Paul McKenna and Dougray Scott for being my companions (and entertainment) on the flight during which the idea for this book was born.

♦ Robert Kirby for submitting the proposal before the ink had dried (twice!)

♦ Michelle Pilley, Julie Oughton, Leanne Siu Anastasi, Margarete Nielsen, Reid Tracy, and the entire Hay House team for proving time and again that business and pleasure are two sides of the same coin. Special mention to Randy Stuart for yet another wonderful cover design!

♦ Lizzie Henry for being the best midwife any literary creation could ever hope to have guiding its entry into the world.

♦ Lynne Robertson, Annette Watling, Joe and Terri Alamo, and Jessica Kulik for doing such a wonderful job of taking care of me and my business while I take time to learn and coach and teach and write.

♦ My best friend, David Beeler, for listening and listening and listening some more as I teased out the stories and themes that fill these pages.

♦ Kristen Mansheim for both her supercoaching and her super-feedback on some early drafts of the first edition of this manuscript.

♦ I have learned so much about these principles from so many, but very special thanks are due to Syd Banks, Dicken Bettinger, Keith Blevens, Cathy Casey, Robin Charbit, Mark Howard, Mavis Karn, Sandy Krot, Ken Manning, Ami Chen Mills-Naim, Roger Mills, Valda Monroe, George Pransky, Jack Pransky, and Elsie Spittle for teaching me more about life in the last 10 years than I'd learned in the first 40.

And most especially to Nina, Oliver, Clara, and Maisy – you are the greatest gifts in my life, and I am truly blessed to get to spend my days with each one of you!

RESOURCES

There is a metaphor in the Zen tradition that in order to truly learn something, we must first swallow the whole fish. The rest of our learning involves 'spitting out the bones' – separating out the insights and good ideas of others from our own wisdom. Since I wrote the original version of this book, well over a hundred new books have been published about the three principles Syd Banks first articulated back in the 1970s. As it can be a bit overwhelming to navigate the sheer volume of live and multimedia offerings now available, I've created a listing of some of my favorites on my website at:

www.michaelneill.org/supercoach

I've also included recommended books, online programs, and live trainings for those of you interested in transformative coaching as a profession. You can visit our special training resource site at:

www.supercoachacademy.com

If you'd like to get in touch with me, you may contact me by email at: michael@michaelneill.org.

While I can't respond personally to every email, please know that I do read everything that is sent!